I dedicate this book to my mom and also in loving memory of my dad (Pops). Your love and support throughout the years has made me into the man that I have become. I love you both more than you know.

I also dedicate this book to the staff of the Orlando House Of Prayer. Your sacrificial love and service to Jesus truly provokes me. I am blessed to serve our Lord alongside you. I am honored to be considered your leader. You guys are the reason OHOP is successful. You truly have blessed my life. Thank You!

Acknowledgments

First and foremost, above all, I would like to thank God for encountering my life in 1981. Without His salvation, this book would never have been written in the first place.

I want to thank my wife Emily and the rest of my family (Jordan, Alexia, Taylor, Landon, Sierra, Matt, Isaac & Caden) who supported and encouraged me, in spite of all the time it took me away from them, as I sat on the back porch of our house for all those months. I am so blessed to be related to you on this side of eternity.

I want to thank my pastor and spiritual father, Benny Hinn, for recognizing the call of God on my life and giving me the opportunity to serve under his leadership. I am forever grateful.

I am full of gratitude and thankfulness to Mike Bickle. Your friendship and constant encouragement over the years and your teachings, leadership, and example of Christ have truly marked my life.

Giving a huge thank you to Lenny Laguardia and Stuart Greaves. You guys have been true friends to me throughout the ministry transition.

I want to thank the senior leadership from IHOP-KC (too many to number) who have poured into our ministry year after year and have strengthened the work here in Central Florida and throughout our beloved state. The many one-on-one conversations have been such a blessing to us.

Thank you Martha Bootle, Karen Shipley, and Stefanie Hauser for your labor of love in helping to edit the book. I pray God blesses you big time.

Adam Grason, thank you for your work of excellence and eagerness to design the book cover. I truly love you, brother.

A special thank you to Chyrl Watts and Marsha Bridgeman for the countless hours you both put into proofreading and editing this project. Without a doubt, this book would not have materialized if it were not for your passion to see this come about. You both inspired me.

Table of Contents

Section Six:
Intercessions Power– "Lord, Show Me How To Get Ready"

Foreword

by Mike Bickle

C arlos and his wife, Emily, give leadership to the Orlando House of Prayer Missions Base in Central Florida. In 2006, Carlos shared with me his encounter with the Lord—calling him to be a forerunner. This is an inspiring prophetic story Carlos shares in Chapter One.

Our two ministries have enjoyed a good relationship and mutual respect for each other as we have worked together to see the prayer movement spread across the earth. The message in this encounter is that the Lord is preparing the Church to embrace a great move of the Holy Spirit. He is raising up sons and daughters who will serve His purposes in their generation.

In this book, Carlos captures the core values in the Kingdom, bringing clarity to the identity of the Church and her calling in partnership with the Lord. The highest identity of the redeemed throughout eternity is to be a "house of prayer" (Isaiah 56:7). This book is filled with practical wisdom that will draw people into connection with God's heart and purpose, so they may be equipped to more effectively partner with what He is doing on the earth in this generation. The greatest revival in history is surely coming. We look with confidence to God's promise in His word to pour out His Spirit, empowering His people to bring the Gospel to all nations.

> "It shall come to pass in the last days, says God, that I will pour out of My Spirit on all flesh; Your sons and your daughters shall prophesy, your young men shall see visions, your old men shall dream dreams . . . I will pour out My Spirit in those days; and they shall prophesy . . . before the coming of the great and awesome day of the LORD."
>
> —*Acts 2:17-20*

In this hour, the Spirit is orchestrating a holy convergence of the missions movement and the prayer movement across the nations. This convergence will flow out of sacred intimacy with Jesus. Loving God is the first priority on God's heart; it always has been and always will be (Matthew 22:37-38). Jesus clarifies that cultivating love for Him is the first commandment, or the first emphasis of the Spirit in our lives. Loving God is a glorious end unto itself; however, it never ends with loving God, but always overflows with loving others. This book has insight that can mark your life and ministry, so take time to read it prayerfully. The encounter Carlos shares will shed new light on walking in unity with God's heart and ways.

—*Mike Bickle International House of Prayer Kansas City*

Preface

The Church is continually being bombarded and challenged by society and the culture as to her faith and her ability to impact the peoples of the earth. Unless the Church becomes a viable voice in this day and hour, she forfeits her prophetic anointing and ability to speak to the ills and moral decay corrupting the nations. Therefore, it is urgent that we, as individual believers and as a corporate spiritual body, learn to walk intimately with the God of Heaven, through the Person of the Holy Spirit.

Throughout Scripture, we are told God's Spirit is continually speaking to the Church to make her increasingly aware of God's will and plan to manifest Himself in the earth. However, when the Church is too occupied with her own will, she leaves no room for God's Spirit to effectively communicate the will of Heaven through the heart of the Church. Jesus made it clear His Father would send the Holy Spirit to us after His resurrection from the dead and subsequent ascension into Heaven. It is the Holy Spirit's work to continuously reveal the will of the Father to the Church. John 14:26 reveals this truth:

> "But the Helper, the Holy Spirit, whom the Father will send in My name, He will teach you all things, and bring to your remembrance all things that I said to you."

The Church has a desperate need to once again learn to hear, with clarity, the voice of God. We must recognize His voice to comprehend His will. Only by receiving the revelation of God's Word through daily dependence upon His presence and pursuit of His face, will we become enabled to follow the Lord as He guides us into all truth. Voices are clamoring loudly, demanding to be heard from various directions within the culture, so we must intentionally tune our spiritual ears to hear God. Moreover, we must be willing to turn off and tune out thousands of voices seeking to distract us, keeping us from being a presence-led people.

Nations of the earth need a people who know God and know His voice, those who can clearly articulate the agenda of the Kingdom of God to their generation. The earth needs to hear a collective voice compelling people to receive the grace and love of God, while simultaneously lifting up the trumpet of God to warn those who choose not to obey the Gospel of Christ. We have, unfortunately, allowed the influences of this age to deafen our ability to hear the voice of our God in sweet communion. Time alone with Him is imperative, if we are to be an effective reflection of His voice in the earth.

It is for this reason I have felt compelled by the Lord to write this book, which came out of an experience I had with the Lord on May 8, 2005. Since then, the Lord has brought me on a journey and has encountered my heart over and over again, more and more deeply, preparing me to be a vessel He could use in this day and hour as one of His prophetic voices. The Lord began to graciously show me I had been drifting into a version of comfortable Christianity, but, in all honesty, I was somewhat aware of it. After serving the Lord in full-time ministry for over nineteen years (1986-2005) and seeing great success, both on the evangelistic field and in the birthing of a new church, it was difficult for me to perceive how I could respond to a deeper life of consecration to the Lord, without having to sacrifice something I had worked very hard to achieve for Him. Fruit was abundant in this ministry of the Lord, but the reality was, if I truly desired newer and better wine, I would first have to prepare the wineskin of my heart to handle the freshness of His Spirit pressing in on me.

I was stuck in my own way of thinking about the manner in which ministry should be accomplished. I did not realize I was too dull of hearing to follow the Spirit's leading and direction in this day and hour. Hearing Him is at the core of being a prophetic people, having the ability to hear what God is currently doing, without devaluing what He did in the past. I had to realize that because I was primarily feasting on yesterday's manna, I was actually depriving myself of the fresh manna of God's revelation, His word, and His will for my life. If all we do is live on yesterday's revelation, eventually our experiences and past encounters with God will not be able to sustain us throughout the pressures coming against our faith in the days and years ahead. We must not make monuments or trophies of our spiritual experiences in God or what He has accomplished in us and through us in our past.

Our hearts must continually be attentive to the fresh blowing of the winds of the Spirit, and our sails must always be open, to be filled with the currents of God's breath, so He may lead and guide us in the way we are to go. The younger generations need to see the present older generation exemplify what it is to truly live a surrendered life, to fulfill the purposes of God, and to establish the Kingdom of our Lord in our midst.

As I share in the first chapter of the book about God encountering me in May 2005, you will see how this visitation became the impetus to a fresh understanding of the importance of always remaining pliable and tenderhearted to the voice of God. This is essential, being always positioned to hear and know His will. God desires to fill a prophetic generation, not only carrying out prophetic declarations from prophets of the past, but also hearing and proclaiming His purposes as He speaks today.

> "'And it shall come to pass in the last days,' says God, 'That I will pour out of My Spirit on all flesh; Your sons and your daughters shall prophesy, Your young men shall see visions, Your old men shall dream dreams.'"
>
> —*Acts 2:17*

This is the hour of encounters with the Holy Spirit, as the Father is beginning to release His presence and power within the Church, to prepare and qualify her to be the vessel He will use to bring in the greatest harvest and manifestation of God's anointing the earth has ever seen. This is an hour of restoration, in which the Holy Spirit is renewing fundamental truths in the life of the Church, so she may be strengthened to build upon the proper foundation, to withstand the forces of deception seeking to paralyze her from walking in the fullness of all she is called to be today.

This is the hour God's Spirit is encountering ordinary individuals from diverse backgrounds, both in ministry and in the marketplace, that He may fill them with His prophetic anointing and raise them up to be end-time, prophetic messengers who will speak the truth of God with boldness and great humility. Men and women everywhere, both young and old, are being visited by the Spirit of prophecy, for the sole purpose of restoring the Church to her former glory. God so greatly desires to encounter us once again, revealing Himself as the God of intimacy and the God of all grace. Jesus will have a Church, walking in her bridal identity and carrying upon herself a spirit of justice, releasing the power of God throughout the nations of the earth. These are exciting days in which we find ourselves living, and the Lord has granted you who are reading this book the opportunity to walk as close to His heart as any of the great Bible characters ever did. He has also purposed for each of us to walk in power and authority, as did many of God's prophets during times past. This is an hour of great restoration. Let us hear what the Spirit is saying to the Church today, and let us fix our hearts toward Him, allowing Him to have His way in us.

> "If anyone has ears to hear, let him hear." Then He said to them, "Take heed what you hear. With the same measure you use, it will be measured to you; and to you who hear, more will be given."
>
> —*Mark 4:23-24*

> "Whom heaven must receive until the times of restoration of all things, which God has spoken by the mouth of all His holy prophets since the world began."
>
> —*Acts 3:21*

> "Behold, I stand at the door and knock. If anyone hears My voice and opens the door, I will come in to him and dine with him, and he with Me. To him who overcomes I will grant to sit with Me on My throne, as I also overcame and sat down with My Father on His throne. He who has an ear, let him hear what the Spirit says to the Churches."
>
> —*Revelation 3:20-22*

Section One:
The Heavenly Encounter & Revelations From God

The church was growing, financially we were blessed, souls were being reached and numerous people were being healed. Everything changed in just one night.

One encounter with God in May 2005 shook everything at its core.

"What is going on?" is what I was thinking, as the angel picked me up out of bed. Then, suddenly, my eyes were opened to what was in the heart of God.

Chapter One

My Encounter With God Changed Everything

It was a season when I knew the Lord was trying to communicate something to me. I knew this, because I was feeling disquieted. The feelings were accompanied by a sense of unsettling; these sensing's bombarded my soul for several weeks. It felt like a constant burden, leaving me bewildered, with no idea how I should respond.

I kept pleading, "Lord, I know something is not right within me. Would you please show me what you are trying to say to me?"

In late 2004, I knew a shift was coming, but I did not have a clue what the shift was or when it was coming. I did recognize, however, the same internal disturbance and agitation I had experienced during previous times when God had been preparing me for a seasonal change. He would stir me inside, and I would feel a strong sense of unsettling within my heart and mind.

I thought, perhaps it was time to surrender the church to one of my associate pastors, though everything happening in the natural would have argued against it. We had launched a church plant, early in the year 2000, with a small group of people, and were holding a weekly Bible study. The Lord had spoken to my wife and I about starting a church. We began to take steps of faith towards this vision. After receiving confirmation from key leaders in the Body of Christ, our spiritual covering, Emily's parents and mine, and, most importantly, after getting the go-ahead from the Lord Himself, we made plans to hold our first church service on Resurrection Day, April 23, 2000.

Our first meeting was held in a movie theater with ninety-seven people in attendance. Within a few short years, we were running three weekly services, with five hundred members attending at least one of our weekly ministry meetings. The church was experiencing incredible growth. Souls were being saved, hundreds of homeless and needy families were being fed, those in demonic bondage were being set free, and bodies were being healed of all kinds of sicknesses and diseases. I want to emphasize that what the Lord was doing in our midst was truly glorious and very exciting!

Our congregation purchased twenty-three acres of property, and we had several hundred thousands of dollars in the church's cash reserve accounts. Nevertheless, I knew in my heart there was something more, something deeper, God had for me. My lack of clarity about what I was sensing left me seriously considering leaving the church to the associates and committing myself back into the evangelistic ministry.

2005: A YEAR OF PROPHETIC SHAKING

In February 2005, I attended a prophetic conference here in Orlando, FL, held at Bishop Mark Chironna's church (which, at that time, was called The Master's Touch, now called Church on the Living Edge). Bishop Mark had Prophet Kim Clement in to minister for a few days at his church, and he had invited me to attend the event, and had even graciously offered to have a seat reserved for me up front. I had never seen Kim Clement minister in person, but, I had heard many good things about him; I was really excited to attend one of his meetings!

In one of the evening services, he said he had a prophetic word for somebody in the service who was somehow connected to a family in the state of Indiana. On the surface, it seemed to be a pretty general word, but as Clement spoke the word of knowledge, we witnessed about eleven or twelve people respond to that word. He had each one raise his or her hand to verify family in Indiana. I, personally, did not have any immediate family living in Indiana, but my wife, Emily, who is from Indiana, still had sisters living there. I thought to myself, "It surely cannot be me, because all these people have their hands up, and I don't have anyone in Indiana who is directly connected to me from my immediate family."

Kim Clement went through each individual person who had a hand raised, telling them his prophetic word did not apply to any of them. He then turned to his right, by the right side of the platform, stretched out his hand, pointed in my direction, and said, "It's somebody here in this section. You have somebody connected with Indiana." I felt obligated to raise my hand at that moment, and he authoritatively exclaimed, "It's you!"

Kim went on to prophesy over me, "Young man, take four steps toward this platform. One, two, three, four," he counted them as I took them. "STOP! For, thus says the Lord, 'You have taken four major steps in ministry, but the next one will be the biggest step ever. It will take you to the place where you have dreamt. For the miraculous will flow out of you like water! Like Peter, God is releasing a faith in you to walk on water. Tens of thousands of young people will be touched by your steps of obedience.'"

I was rocked by the prophetic word! I thought to myself, "This is what I need! I know God has something for me in this hour."

I left that service without any clear direction, but I knew the Lord would soon release further revelation to me. I began to seek the Lord by giving myself to more time in prayer, asking for His direction and guidance. I was willing to do anything and go anywhere, as long as I knew it was His leading and His will. Over the next couple of weeks, I began to think about it all, developing my own interpretation as to what I felt the prophetic word could mean for my life.

Having served under Benny Hinn, as one of his pastors for nine years (1986-1995), I had been trained in an atmosphere of the supernatural and was blessed to have worshiped God in incredible revival services. I saw miracles, by the power of God, working through Pastor Benny in a way I had never seen before through any other individual. His ministry and generosity toward my life allowed me to become familiar with the Person of the Holy Spirit, His anointing, and the operation of His power and spiritual gifts. It was truly one of the greatest experiences in all my life. Therefore, when Kim Clement prophesied the supernatural was about to be released in my life in a way I had never dreamed, and it would have an effect on tens of thousands of young people, I began to imagine myself becoming the "Benny Hinn" for the younger generation. I mean, how else might this have been interpreted, other than my traveling as a healing evangelist and seeing tens of thousands of young people impacted by God's power and His healing anointing?

After three months had passed, I began to feel agitation again and was wondering, "What is my next step? How can I begin to fulfill the word Kim had given to me?"

Without my realizing it, Kim's prophetic word helped me position my heart to receive the direction of the Lord for my life and for my family, as well as for our ministry.

THE HEAVENLY ENCOUNTER OF MAY 8, 2005

The answer to all my searching came through an encounter I had in the early morning hours of May 8, 2005. I was awakened out of a deep sleep; when suddenly, I realized my spirit man was coming out of my physical body. I was actually suspended over our bed, and I could see myself lying next to my wife, that is, our physical bodies. "How could this be?" I thought to myself. "What in the world is going on?"

It was then I realized I was not just floating on my own over our bed, but I could feel very strong arms actually cradling me, while I was looking down upon my bed. Once the thought occurred to me, I recognized it was an angel who had stepped into our bedroom and somehow was able to hold me in his arms, while at the same time allowing me to see myself lying there in the bed. He began to rise, and I vividly remember thinking we were going to bump our heads against the ceiling. I closed my eyes and ducked, to avoid hitting the ceiling, but to my surprise, we went right through the roof of the house.

For a moment, I thought, "Somehow, I must have passed away in the night." I began to offer prayers for my wife, Emily, and for each of our five children. I asked the Lord to comfort them and strengthen them in my absence, because I literally thought I had died somehow; my time had come. Suddenly, my heart, from one second to another, was flooded with an incredible sensation of joy and great anticipation, as I realized I was about to go see Jesus! I remember going higher into the atmosphere, going through the clouds and finally coming to a place where I saw no structure of any kind, no building, and no pearly gates. I saw no one as I found myself all alone, standing there in a wide-open expanse. I recall seeing unusual colors. These colors looked as if they were actually breathing and moving. The best way I can describe the scene is this: It was like seeing the colorful jet stream on a weather map from a local television weather report. The experience of seeing the radiant colors seemed so beautifully surreal to me, because I could actually see movement of the colors, as if each was fully alive. I had never seen such beautiful greens, yellows, blues, and reds, and all sorts of other shades. Enjoying the brilliant, rainbow-like kaleidoscope of colors seemed peculiarly new to me, because in the natural, I am colorblind. In that instant, however, I was able to distinguish all varieties of these life-filled colors.

The scene changed abruptly. I suddenly found myself in another open area, where I saw two individuals standing side-by-side at a slight angle. I remember wondering who they were. Suddenly, I realized it was God, the Father and God, the Son. I did not know what to do. Should I fall on my face? Should I run towards them and embrace them, or should I just stay put? Somehow, in my spirit man, I received an impression in my heart, "You have been granted permission to stand and listen."

With that, I fixed my gaze and my attention towards the conversation Jesus was having with the Father. As I listened, I realized communication was filled with information about God's work on the earth, the difficult hour that lay ahead, and the divine plan to use the Church to impact the earth with the Kingdom of God.

My ears perked up, and I began to listen even more intently. I was spellbound as I witnessed the Godhead discussing the end times, with its forthcoming rise of the antichrist spirit, as well as its effect on the nations of the earth. They talked about the persecution of the Church and the great hour of trial and suffering the earth is yet to see. It was then I began to specifically recollect the books of Daniel and Revelation. Long ago, I had done a few studies on eschatology, but the subject was no longer an emphasis of mine. Jesus and His Father had captured my absolute concentration; I somehow began to sense the urgency in the conversation; the events mentioned could actually take place in my lifetime, during my generation. In the midst of speaking, the Father looked at the Son and said the most terrifying words I had ever heard:

He said, "It's time, Son; Go get Your Bride!"

I tell you, they were truly the most horrifying words I had ever heard. It was as if I had been given an instant download, along with immediate understanding as to what it meant. I stood there, realizing those words meant Jesus would be coming for His Bride, His Church! I began to feel the weight of the reality of my own heart, unprepared for His return. Those words, "Go get Your Bride," burst forth from the Father's mouth like a ball of fire. I could literally see the words, as they rolled towards me, and they struck me in my midsection. Immediately, the living Words caused my body to tremble and shake violently. I felt something in my stomach, rising up into my chest area, and something came into my throat. I raised both of my arms up over my head and shook them violently, while crying out loudly from my spirit man, "No! We are not ready!!!"

I remember thinking to myself, "Oh! What did I just say? Why did I say that?"

It was too late to think of taking back my cry; the words had already escaped my lips, with a cry of desperation, from a heart requiring more time to prepare before the coming of the Lord.

With great regret, I lowered my head in shame, as I wondered how much I must have disappointed the Lord. I had just revealed my heart before Him; even I now recognized my state of unpreparedness. I finally found the courage to lift up my head; I looked again towards the Father and the Son. Suddenly, over my left shoulder, I heard another Voice, saying in both an authoritative and gentle manner, "I know the ones who are ready."

In an instant, like the flash of the blink of an eye, my spirit man was back in my natural body.

This time I was no longer on the bed, but I was on the floor to the side of the bed, curled up on my knees, my body in the shape of a ball.

When I came to my natural senses, I found myself inhaling deeply, as if breath and physical life had just returned to my body. I could still feel the effects of the Father's words, as I realized where I was, and I could feel an intense heat going up and down and throughout my body. I could not contain my emotions. I remember putting my hands on my head, with my face lifted up, crying out, "My God, my God, what was that? What was that?"

I looked at the clock for a moment, realizing it was 4:00 in the morning; my senses were becoming more focused as to my natural surroundings.

I looked over to the bed. Emily was still there, sleeping. I got myself up and went to the bonus room in our home. I threw myself onto the floor there, where I lay for two hours, weeping, trembling, and feeling completely perplexed. Anguished thoughts of the words I had spoken in that heavenly encounter, "No, we are not ready!" filled my mind during those two hours. I kept asking the Lord to forgive me for saying such words. I was certain I had greatly displeased Him. My mind was flooded with questions: "Why would I say that in the first place? Could it be I somehow had deceived myself? Was I actually not ready to meet with God in eternity?"

My own thoughts were racing now, concerning what He had spoken to me: "Is this referring to my entire family not being fully prepared or in the right spiritual place in our service of the Lord? Did that encounter expose the heart of the ministry we were overseeing? Was the Lord somehow trying to communicate that we were not rightly focused in doing the work of God?"

All these questions flooded my mind at once, bringing me more fear and consternation. I finally cried out to the Lord, "Jesus, I don't know what to do. I don't know how to prepare myself. Please help me be prepared for Your coming."

Immediately, I heard the gentle, comforting Holy Spirit. He responded, "Son, if I were to take you home right now, you are ready to meet Me in eternity, but the condition of your heart right now, you are not ready for the next great move of My Spirit with which I'm about to visit the earth."

For an instant, I was simultaneously relieved and dismayed. Relieved, because my heart was right before God, after all, in reference to my salvation. Though, in my heart, I truly believed I was in right standing in my relationship with the Lord, I was being shaken in that moment. I began to waver and question my position in Him. My encounter with the Lord, though, had nothing to do with my eternal position or my righteous stance before Him, through Jesus. That was a settled matter, a done deal. However, the Holy Spirit was definitely highlighting something in my heart, but I couldn't yet comprehend. Pondering His final statement to me, a feeling of self-justification began to rise up in me. I thought to myself, "How can it be? I'm doing all this for You, Lord. The church is growing, great things are happening, and the Holy Spirit is manifesting His power in our midst."

I guess it really disturbed me to think I, personally, might not be ready for the next move of God's power on the earth, especially since I had come from a Holy Spirit empowered ministry. After a bit more time, just lying there, contemplating, I resolved to come into agreement with the Lord.

I cried out, "Lord, then teach me how to get ready!"

I got up off the floor, committed to allow the Lord to do whatever He wanted to do in me. My prayer life increased again, in an effort to discover exactly how to get ready for whatever the Lord wanted to do.

About two weeks passed, and I received a flyer in the mail that read, "International House of Prayer: End-Time Prophetic Conference." Somehow, I had been placed on their mailing list. The theme of their conference really spoke to me. As I stared at the flyer, the voice of the Lord rang loudly and clearly, "Go there; I will give you instruction as to what to do next."

I asked my secretary to register me for the prophetic conference and to book me a flight to Kansas City. Arriving in Kansas City in June 2005, my heart was filled with eager anticipation. I had a sense of expectancy; I knew God was going to encounter me to bring clarity to this whole prophetic swirl of an encounter, but exactly what or how, I had no idea.

THE REVELATION OF THE FORERUNNER CALLING

At the site of the conference, I tried to find a seat as close as possible to the front of the auditorium. Having never been there before, I did not know how many people to expect or the size of their meeting room. To my utter surprise, as I arrived several minutes before the start of the service, I found the building pretty much packed out. I settled for a seat all the way in the back. The moment the worship service began, I was completely undone. I felt the presence of the Lord all over me, as I began to perceive I was in a room filled with lovesick people, in hot pursuit of their God. I could not recall ever having been part of such a hungry, thirsty-for-God crowd of worshipers. I'd been in services with a much larger number of people before, even in the midst of people hungry for the power of God, but this was different, as there seemed to be a spirit of unity all the way from the platform and throughout the congregation. They were all in agreement, as they were there mainly for one thing: to encounter God's presence and to be more in love with Him.

I was struck by the depth of the worship in which Misty Edwards, (main worship leader for International House Of Prayer), led the congregation. It was such a breath of fresh air, like jumping into the purest, most refreshing pool of water. When worship was over, and Mike Bickle began to teach, I was struck again by the depth of the Word. Suddenly, I connected what he was teaching to my personal encounter from three weeks earlier. I began to shake and weep, as I sat there in one of the pews, losing total awareness of where I was. I couldn't help what I was feeling, as I sat there trembling, shaking, and weeping. I tried to hold my composure to the best of my ability.

Suddenly, the voice of the Lord broke through, saying,

"Son, this is your destiny. You have been passionate for Me, and you will continue to be in the days ahead. I am calling you to be one of My forerunners to help me prepare My Bride for My return. My Church is asleep and they do not realize how close My return is. I will send you (one of many) to be a voice of awakening to them and prepare them for Me!"

With that, I cried out in my heart and responded, "Yes! Lord, I want to be one of Your forerunners! Just teach me how to prepare and how to get ready. Show me what to do next!"

THE REVELATION OF THE BRIDE AND THE HOUSE OF PRAYER

During this trip to Kansas City, I spent countless hours in their prayer room, as the Holy Spirit began to give me revelation and understanding as to my identity before Him. He began to unveil to me the truth of the Bridal paradigm and of the Church being called God's house of prayer for all nations. Sitting in a room full of worshipers and intercessors caused my heart to yearn for something like this to occur in Orlando, Florida, as well. IHOP-Kansas City started a night-and-day prayer meeting in September of 1999 that has been perpetually flowing. It has not stopped for one second since its inception. It is a remarkable place. The Tabernacle of David ideal, embraced by leadership and worshipers, has truly mentored our ministry team to go deeper in God. We have more fully understood our prophetic identity before the Lord.

My regular visits to the IHOP-Kansas City prayer room over the years and my time in our own prayer room here in Central Florida have unveiled to me five core values, we have since adopted. These values have formed the foundation of our ministry. Looking back, each core value was revealed to me in the encounter I had with the Lord. I will spend time breaking down each of these core values in the rest of the book:

INTIMACY WITH GOD
KINGDOM LIFESTYLE (CHRISTLIKENESS)
END-TIME URGENCY
LIFE AND POWER IN THE SPIRIT
AUTHORITY OF INTERCESSION

"In 2005, after my director, Carlos Sarmiento, was encountered, my heart began to be awakened to the message he was releasing, 'The message of the Bride of Christ.' Growing up in the church, I had the revelation that God was my Father in Heaven and that He loved me as His daughter. I also knew He was the Judge that was always watching, determining Heaven or hell for me, and a great measure of the fear of the Lord was in me. But I never recall being taught this new message that was striking my heart, 'Andrea, YOU are the Bride of Christ. He desires you and is calling you to govern with Him as His Bride in heavenly places.'

Shortly after, I found myself at our fellowship service on a Sunday, when suddenly, a member of our church barged in, running straight down the center aisle, up to the altar, eagerly waiting to share something with the leader. After he shared, the leader announced, 'Church, we will transition into a time of prayer, because there is an intense riot happening in downtown Orlando!'

Moments after engaging with the corporate cry, I was baptized with tongues, which I had never before experienced. Closing my eyes, I saw a girl standing as a soldier, with a pink Mohawk, dressed in all black, with piercings all over, and very angry. As I groaned, I could feel the pain in God's heart concerning her and the riot. It was almost as if the groaning became Scriptures, and I could see them being released into her and over the city. She went from a solid rock to being on her knees weeping. Instantly, I knew that what was happening through me was shifting something in her heart and over the atmosphere of Orlando. It was in that moment, I clearly heard the invitation of the Lord.

'What if you laid your life down to do this? What if you continued to partner with Me in this way? What if you set yourself apart in body, soul, and spirit? What if you gave up things in this life to prepare a place for Me to come and govern?'

That day, November 8th, marked history made in my heart. It is with great honor that I can confidently say—years after answering that call—there are no regrets, only a greater satisfaction, hunger, and understanding. It was and still is a call released not only to me and to our community, but it was also the call released to the generations gone before us. Yet again, we have the opportunity to answer that call, to forcefully advance the Kingdom, to be separate as the Bride who eagerly awaits Her Beloved, making right the greatest injustice ever known on earth, that which lies in ruins, desecrated and void; restoring His holy sanctuary, His dwelling place, His presence on the earth. The facts are that our generation is unsatisfied with everything around her. Her heart testifies of the true longing of the human heart—the longing for His return."

—Andrea Caraballo Full-time Intercessory Missionary
Orlando House of Prayer

Chapter Two

Key Heart Issues
God Is Emphasizing

Having been encountered by the Lord so powerfully and given insight into the burden of His heart, I began to seek Him like I never had before. On several previous occasions, the Holy Spirit had encountered me with His presence, but this time was absolutely immeasurably overwhelming. I knew the Lord wanted to reveal areas of my own heart and life, which were not meeting His Kingdom standards. Shaken to the core, I sought the Lord for His precise plan and His exact focus for my life. Over and over again, I would find myself sitting; simply pondering my encounter with the Lord, until I slowly but distinctly began to identify His prophetic message stirring within me. He desired for me to perceive His communication with clarity. I was to be deeply impacted by His revelation and would begin to articulate His burden to the Body of Christ at large.

Not only did I come face-to-face with issues in my own heart, but I also began to see key heart issues the Church must deal with in this day and hour, if she is to be a relevant voice in a confused and dark world. Unless we are able to hear the voice of the Holy Spirit, we will not be equipped or qualified to speak the heart of God clearly to the complacent Church or to those utterly devoid of the knowledge of God.

The first thing the Holy Spirit began to show me was the most critical need in the Church today. The Church includes you and me, as individual believers, in addition to the corporate Body of Christ. Primarily, the Church needs leaders who allow their own hearts to be encountered by the Lord. The Church must encounter first-hand experience and discipleship from pastors and other five-fold leaders, who are completely surrendered to the will of God and His manifestation in their ministries. However, it is impossible, unless the hearts of these leaders are yielded to fulfilling the great commandment. Unfortunately, we leaders get too heavily bogged down in the work of the ministry, as if this is what He requires of us, as if our methods alone are pleasing to Him. It is true, the Lord, by His Spirit, releases to us the mandate for our lives and ministries, but workload must never replace the great commandment of knowing and loving God. What the Church of Jesus Christ needs today is radical, love-sick, ministers of God.

1. Intimacy With The Eternal Godhead

If we are going to fulfill the plan God has for our lives and do so with joy and assurance of bringing Him pleasure, we must return our hearts to the very place God intended them to be forever! One day in the eternal Kingdom of God, our hearts will be forever His. Until that day comes, our hearts must long for His presence and must yearn to abide with Him regularly on this side of eternity. Jesus is not looking for believers who feel obligated to spend time with Him in order to please Him. Spiritual disciplines of prayer, worship, Bible reading, Bible study, church attendance, and the sharing of our faith have far greater purpose. There is no doubt these spiritual disciplines offer tremendous benefit to our lives in and of themselves. More than rote practices, though, God longs to see His people come to Him voluntarily. He wants us to desire Him as much as He desires us. This is the beautiful opportunity given to mankind. Regardless of our weaknesses and frailties, He, by His own power and grace, is able to touch the human heart, creating a burning passion to love and pursue God.

> "For it is God who works in you both to will and to do for His good pleasure."
>
> —*Philippians 2:13*

Throughout Scripture, God reveals Himself as a God of love and a God who longs to be approached by His creation. The very purpose of Jesus' coming was to demystify the assumption that God could not be known. He lived and died and rose again to connect mankind to the Father, to declare God's love and willingness to be revealed and encountered. Jesus Himself said He came to manifest the Father to those who followed and believed in Him.

"I have manifested Your name to the men whom You have given Me out of the world. They were Yours, You gave them to Me, and they have kept Your word."

—John 17:6

"And I have declared to them Your name, and will declare it, that the love with which You loved Me may be in them, and I in them."

—John 17:26

It is for this reason: Jesus paid the ultimate price by going to the Cross at Calvary. In doing so, He made it possible for those who would put their trust in Him to become one with God. Our faith in Christ opens the door for us to have a spiritual union, much like the relationship between a husband and wife. The ceremony of holy matrimony creates the miracle of taking two individuals and making them one in spirit, one in soul, and one in body. This has been God's eternal purpose and consuming desire since the foundations of the earth. All of Scripture and all of God's plans culminate in this one purpose: the desire for God and man to become one.

This was the great revelation the Holy Spirit had revealed to the Apostle Paul. Paul understood the metaphor between Christ and His Church becoming one, just as a man and a woman join together in marriage. No other work of God is greater than this. Everything else God did, and ever will do, comes back around to the purpose of fulfilling His eternal desire for mankind.

"That they all may be one, as You, Father, are in Me, and I in You; that they also may be one in Us that the world may believe that You sent Me."

—John 17:21

"For we are members of His body, of His flesh and of His bones. 'For this reason a man shall leave his father and mother and be joined to his wife, and the two shall become one flesh.' This is a great mystery, but I speak concerning Christ and the Church."

—Ephesians 5:30-32

Beginning with the book of Genesis, where we see the first-ever recorded wedding between Adam and Eve, we are given insight into the heart of God (Genesis 2:21-25). After creating the earth as a place of habitation for His creation, we are taught God's purpose for creating man. God's desire was for man to encounter Him and walk closely with God. Think of it, the God of the universe, the Creator Himself was seeking and desiring to walk intimately with man. Scripture then reveals Jesus' first recorded miracle He ever performed as a human being on the earth: turning water into wine. What's so significant about that? When one takes into consideration the location of the miracle, we again see what's at the very core of God's heart. By doing His first miracle at a wedding in Cana of Galilee, the Holy Spirit is revealing to us the very passion burning in the heart of the eternal Godhead. This speaks clearly of a day when God will save the best wine for last, and all of redeemed humanity will celebrate an eternal union with the wine of joy, love, and eternal intimacy with God (John 2:1-12, Revelation 19:7-9, 21:1-3, 22:17).

Scripture continues to expound on this revelation: the Apostle John, as recorded in the book of Revelation, received, by inspiration of the Holy Spirit, a prophetic download depicting the end of the age, culminating with yet another kind of wedding. It will be the greatest wedding ever to be witnessed, not just recorded in Scripture, but the greatest wedding of all time, in all of eternity. John describes the wedding between the Bridegroom—Jesus Christ, the Son of God—and the Bride of Christ—the Church. Hallelujah! What a glorious day that will be!

> "And I heard, as it were, the voice of a great multitude, as the sound of many waters and as the sound of mighty thunderings, saying, 'Alleluia! For the Lord God Omnipotent reigns!'"
>
> —*Revelation 19:6*

2. The Kingdom-Of-God Lifestyle

The second heart issue the Lord revealed to me was the necessity of living with the Kingdom of God at the center of all we think, say, and do, and to prepare our hearts for the return of Christ. During my encounter with the Lord in May 2005, I specifically recall the Father decreeing it was time for Jesus to come and claim His Bride. You might think I would have been, upon hearing these words, jumping for joy. Most of us in the Church respond quite favorably to discussion of Jesus' soon return, for the purpose of receiving us to Himself and establishing His Kingdom on the earth. However, I suppose at the precise moment of my encounter, it was like a revelation beginning to illuminate my heart and mind to the reality of Christ's return. I felt a keen sense of unpreparedness. The Holy Spirit was actually pointing out the measly measure of my heart's consecration to Him and His Kingdom purposes. It was, by far, one of the most terrifying experiences of my life.

To be honest with you, I would not wish such terror on my worst enemy. Fear gripped my heart like I had never known before. As a result of this confrontation, however, I began to understand this premise: Many of us in the Body of Christ develop a prayer life, in which we cry out to God for the primary purpose of receiving more of His blessings and more success in this life. We might even cry out for a greater measure of His power and anointing or for larger ministries. Whatever the case may be, the bottom line is this: Most in the Body of Christ are not seeking the Kingdom of God first, as Jesus so wisely instructed us to do.

> "But seek first the Kingdom of God and His righteousness, and all these things shall be added to you."
>
> —*Matthew 6:33*

This is why God, the Father, has given to us the Person of the Holy Spirit to be our Helper while we are on the earth (John 14:26, 15:26, 16:5-5). The Father knows our tendencies and inclinations to seek after things more beneficial or pleasurable in the natural life, rather than predominantly searching after true spiritual riches to strengthen the inward life. God's Spirit works diligently in our hearts for the specific purpose of predestining us to be sons and daughters of God, who will be conformed into the image of His Son (Romans 8:29, Galatians 4:19, Colossians 1:28). The hope for the nations of the earth is for the Church to exemplify and represent the Kingdom of God effectively, carrying the bloodstained banner of Jesus Christ as an ensign before this dark and hopeless world. When unbelievers see Christians truly devoted to fulfilling God's purposes, rather than living primarily for themselves, sinners will begin to desire the peace and joy overflowing from the hearts of believers. This is the aim of the Holy Spirit. He seeks to raise up a people who will truly live out the great mandate of loving God and keeping His commandments.

> "If you love Me, keep My commandments. And I will pray the Father, and He will give you another Helper, that He may abide with you forever—the Spirit of truth, whom the world cannot receive, because it neither sees Him nor knows Him; but you know Him, for He dwells with you and will be in you. I will not leave you orphans; I will come to you."
>
> *—John 14:15-18*

The Kingdom of God is calling representatives who will be faithful ambassadors. It would do us well to be reminded of the reality: We are not our own. We actually belong to another Kingdom (John 17:15-16, 1 Corinthians 6:20, 7:23). Jesus' death was not intended simply to produce mediocre demonstration of His Kingdom.

An ambassador of Christ may be likened to an ambassador of an earthly country, who lives overseas in another country. He dwells there to represent his country of origin; he communicates his country's agenda on various issues and the position and stance of his government. Likewise, it is critical for us to allow the Holy Spirit to develop the character of Christ and His Kingdom in our hearts, because only then will we be fit to faithfully represent God here on the earth. God's Kingdom is not a natural one at the moment; rather, it is primarily a spiritual Kingdom, dwelling within hearts of redeemed humanity (Luke 17:20-21). However, if our lives are still controlled by the carnal nature, rather than the Holy Spirit's leadership, the power of God's Kingdom will be impeded from being fully manifest in and through us.

> "Whoever therefore breaks one of the least of these commandments, and teaches men so, shall be called least in the Kingdom of heaven; but whoever does and teaches them, he shall be called great in the Kingdom of heaven. For I say to you, that unless your righteousness exceeds the righteousness of the scribes and Pharisees, you will by no means enter the Kingdom of heaven."
>
> *—Matthew 5:19-20*

3. End-Time Urgency

When we take an internal inspection of the condition of the Church today, it is not difficult to see the complacent attitudes many possess while living out their faith walk with God. One of the paramount reasons for such apathy is simply because the leadership in the Body of Christ has presented only a meager teaching on the doctrine of eschatology: doctrine of the end times, return of Christ, and the establishment of the millennial Kingdom on the earth. Lack of understanding eschatology has left the Church unprepared, without the sense of urgency of the prophetic hour in which we live.

Over and over again, throughout the Gospels, Jesus warned His disciples (Matthew 24:42-43, 25:13, Mark 13:33-37, Luke 21:36) to ensure they were being watchful and ready for His return. Whether or not we are living in a state of expectancy, our daily decisions for our lives reflect what we truly believe concerning the second coming of our Lord. Like the saying goes, "Out of sight, out of mind." The reality is this: If Jesus is not at the center of our thoughts and desires, our minds and hearts will be elsewhere. It is no wonder, today we have believers in Christ all across the nations of the earth, especially in Western society, whose hearts are weighed down with cares of this life. What a great shock it will be to those believers who are alive at the coming of the Lord, when, at His return, they will not be found watching and waiting.

> "But take heed to yourselves, lest your hearts be weighed down with carousing, drunkenness, and cares of this life, and that Day come on you unexpectedly. For it will come as a snare on all those who dwell on the face of the whole earth. Watch therefore, and pray always that you may be counted worthy to escape all these things that will come to pass, and to stand before the Son of Man."
>
> —*Luke 21:34-36*

The Apostle Paul spent a good amount of his ministry time making sure his disciples and the churches he had established would be well grounded in eschatology (1 Corinthians 15:50-58, 1 Timothy 4:1-3, 2 Timothy 3:1-5, 1 Thessalonians 4:13-18, 5:1-11, 2 Thessalonians 1:1-11). This is probably one of the most neglected doctrinal teachings today. It is for this reason, once again, the Holy Spirit is reemphasizing the need for the Church to teach on the doctrine of eschatology.

Like Paul, leaders of the Church today must focus on preparing God's people for the difficult days ahead. We must ensure the Church is being confidently grounded in the teaching of the end times. The Body of Christ must know perfectly well, the day of the Lord comes like a thief in the night (1 Thessalonians 5:2-3). Sadly, many who are unprepared will be saying in an unaware state of mind, "There is peace and safety," only to experience the reality of destruction coming upon the earth suddenly, just as labor pains come upon a woman who is with child. Those who do not know the Lord will not be able to escape that day, but the Church is not meant to be in darkness, nor is that day intended to overtake His Beloved as a thief in the night.

As the Day of the Lord approaches, God's Spirit will raise up prophetic forerunners, both male and female, young and old, in high numbers, who will have given themselves completely to becoming His extravagant servants, who will prepare the way for the second coming of the Lord. Much like Elijah and John the Baptist, these prophetic, end-time messengers will actually carry upon themselves a very strong prophetic spirit to diligently prepare God's people for His return. Those who choose to become consecrated and prepared will be those whom God will anoint, so they may reach out to lost society and declare the approach of God's soon-coming Kingdom.

> "For he will be great in the sight of the Lord, and shall drink neither wine nor strong drink. He will also be filled with the Holy Spirit, even from his mother's womb. And he will turn many of the children of Israel to the Lord their God. He will also go before Him in the spirit and power of Elijah, 'to turn the hearts of the fathers to the children,' and the disobedient to the wisdom of the just, to make ready a people prepared for the Lord."
>
> *—Luke 1:15-17*

"Decades ago, worshiping at my piano, I was singing my love to God, when suddenly, I heard God's Spirit begin to sing over me the very lyrics I'd been singing to Him. It was my voice bringing forth the sound, but I knew His Spirit had overshadowed me and shaken me to the core, like I'd never experienced before. He replaced His name, embedded in the lyrics, with mine: 'Marsha, what a wonder you are. You are so gentle, so pure, and so kind. You shine like the morning star. Marsha, what a wonder you are.' Immediately following, I broke into deep, uncontrollable sobs. From the depths of my being I was shaking, as I cried out, 'No, Jesus! You are! No way I'm like that. No way.'

I remember His reply as if it were yesterday: 'That's the way I see you, through the sacrifice of My blood, shed for you.'

I'm not sure I believed Him at that point, but His divine love—in that moment—had captured my heart, had captivated me in the midst of my personal desperation. He came and poured on me what I needed most. In my brokenness, His fiery eyes looked right through me, and I knew I was loved. God Himself loved me. God! Loved! Me! He was establishing His Secret Place in me. From that day forward, I became increasingly aware of a God, the Creator and Possessor of Heaven and earth, the God of the universe, the Supreme Chief Justice; this same God was in pursuit of me, to display His love for me. He and I have exchanged love songs ever since.

He loves thoroughly. He loves perfectly. His love knows no bounds. His love has no end. His love is pure. His love is faithful. His love is true. His love is relentless. His love is matchless. No one loves like this Man. He has taken me on a life-long journey with Him, to comprehend the incomprehensible: the height, the depth, the breadth, and the length of a love that has no boundaries. Sounds complicated, even impossible. Throughout eternity, we will be exploring the vastness and the beauty of this Man and His love.

Singing my love songs, weekly, in the OHOP prayer room, my heart has been exponentially strengthened in Him. As deep keeps calling unto deep, I've entered the Secret Place, but under the OHOP corporate anointing for continual prayer and worship, I've experienced increasing depths of revelation from this Man, my Jehovah Nissi, the Lord, my banner, whose victory over me is His love. In the Secret Place, heart-to-heart and face-to-face, transformation takes place, as He reveals the mysteries of God. I'm in Him, and He's in me. He's jealous for me, and He makes war against anything that hinders love. He will have a purified Bride to reign with Him and partner with Him to establish His Kingdom, on earth, as it is in Heaven. I thank God for the OHOP people and prayer room, but I am eternally grateful for my home, the Secret Place of the Most High God."

—*Marsha Bridgeman*
Worship leader Orlando House of Prayer

Chapter Three

It Is Time To Do & Manifest the Kingdom

In the previous chapter, we discussed three key heart issues in the Church with which God's Holy Spirit is dealing. If the Church is to be positioned correctly, she must yield to the working of the Holy Spirit to become the useful instrument to release God's light and witness in the earth.

This leads us to two key actions the Church must begin to manifest in the hour of great conflict.

THE FIRST PROPHETIC ACTION IS THE NEED TO ONCE AGAIN EXAMINE THE FULLNESS OF THE HOLY SPIRIT, WHICH IS AVAILABLE FOR EACH AND EVERY INDIVIDUAL MEMBER OF THE BODY OF CHRIST.

In my encounter with the Lord, I became greatly disturbed by the things I saw and heard. I remember lying on the floor, weeping before the Lord, asking for insight and understanding. After about two hours of feeling broken and ill-equipped, I heard the Spirit of the Lord speak clearly, and I was thoroughly shaken. He revealed this to me: "You are not ready for the next great move of My Spirit."

I will be honest; at first I was offended at His revelation, since I had been trained under a ministry that believes and operates in the supernatural gifts of the Holy Spirit. I thought to myself, "How is it possible I am not ready for the next move of God's Spirit on the earth?"

The Lord showed me this truth: Although the ministry had witnessed demonstrations of His power in our midst, the condition of my own heart, as well as the condition of the heart of the ministry, was focused on personal advantage, rather than seeking the benefit of the Kingdom of God.

The Holy Spirit began to reveal these principles to me: Great power must be accompanied by great grace upon each and every life. Hearts must be kept pure and humble. All the glory and credit must be offered to Jesus, for the works He will do through us.

Simultaneously, I began to comprehend the countless others in the Body who would not be ready for the Day of the Lord. Lack of understanding the Holy Spirit's role in the end-time scenario would certainly be rampant. This would manifest, because of increasing blindness to the Holy Spirit's desire to minister within individual hearts and lives. Let us focus on this for a moment.

THE POWER OF THE HOLY SPIRIT

It is evident from Scripture, Jesus never intended for the baptism and empowerment of the Holy Spirit to be experienced by only a select few believers. The Word of God is clear enough: Each of us must believe His Spirit is for all who trust in Him (Acts 2:38-39). We each have the right to claim His anointing and His power, so we might learn how to operate in the gifts of the Holy Spirit, as outlined in 1 Corinthians 12. Jesus made it abundantly clear. He came to bring fire upon the earth, a baptism of fire in His Spirit. He would give it to those who believed in Him.

> "I indeed baptize you with water unto repentance, but He who is coming after me is mightier than I, whose sandals I am not worthy to carry. He will baptize you with the Holy Spirit and fire."
>
> —*Matthew 3:11*

The Word of God places great emphasis on the third Person of the Trinity, the Holy Spirit; therefore, we would do well to commit ourselves to studying the Person, the work, and the ministry of the Holy Spirit. The truth is, many believers live their entire Christian lives without ever acknowledging the abiding presence or power of the precious Holy Spirit. Too often, they are unaware of the availability of His presence and power. The secret to Jesus' ministry was in the relationship He had with His Father, through the Holy Spirit. It is the Holy Spirit who reveals Jesus, and He also teaches us and unveils to us the nature and will of God, the Father. If we hunger and thirst for the Lord, we will be led to a greater understanding of Scripture and a deeper comprehension of our One God—in three Persons. Becoming intimately acquainted with the Holy Spirit, we will experience, with greater clarity, His will for, as well as His presence in our lives (John 7:37-39, 14:16-26, 15:26, 16:5-15).

I am actually bewildered when I see so many in the Body of Christ who do not encounter the power of God on a regular basis. Studying the life of Jesus, we notice how dependent He was upon the ministry of the Spirit all His days upon the earth. Jesus Himself relied upon the Spirit's power, anointing, and gifts, and He co-labored in the Spirit's purpose of serving humanity. Throughout the Gospels, on several occasions, we read about the power of God flowing through Jesus' life to bring healing, deliverance, and restoration to the lives He touched. Jesus placed a high emphasis on allowing the Holy Spirit to lead and guide Him in all His speech and actions. Jesus' initiation into ministry perfectly exemplified the level of priority the Holy Spirit must have in the life of every serious believer, especially those of us called to minister The Word of the Lord. We are told in Luke 3-4, immediately after Jesus received the Holy Spirit, following His baptism at the Jordan River, the Spirit of God led Him into the wilderness.

It was in the wilderness, Jesus experienced the temptations of satan, who attempted to distract and detract Him from obeying God's plan for His life. Jesus was filled with both The Word of God and the Holy Spirit, which gave Him the assurance of victory over the enemy (Luke 3:21-22, 4:1-13). Having triumphed victoriously over the wilderness temptation experience, He immediately declared the Spirit of the Lord upon Himself. He declared His Father had anointed Him to preach the Gospel to the poor and to demonstrate the power of God, by healing the brokenhearted, and by bringing deliverance to those held as captives to sin's power. Beloved, how much more, then, do we need the ministry of the Holy Spirit in our own lives and ministries today? Every believer who longs to live an overcoming, fruitful life must be prepared by the Spirit Himself to overcome the enemy in spiritual warfare.

> "Then Jesus went about all the cities and villages, teaching in their synagogues, preaching the Gospel of the Kingdom, and healing every sickness and every disease among the people."
>
> —*Matthew 9:35*

> "How God anointed Jesus of Nazareth with the Holy Spirit and with power, who went about doing good and healing all who were oppressed by the devil, for God was with Him."
>
> —*Acts 10:38*

The exciting thing is this: We all have the opportunity to encounter the Spirit's power and His continual presence upon our lives. The last days will be marked with a people who know the power of God, those who will be well equipped to confront—and contend against—the compromise in the Church, as well as the increasing powers of darkness and iniquity throughout the nations of the earth (Daniel 11:32). We must understand, just as darkness is increasing, like the prophet Isaiah decreed, so righteousness is escalating (Isaiah 60:13). We must press in, to mature in all His fullness, as the Holy Spirit empowers a people to perform His acts of justice in an unjust world. The prophet Joel plainly declared the Church will witness a great demonstration of power and might at the closing hour, just prior to the coming of the Lord. The Apostle Peter reiterated and confirmed this prophecy, in Acts 2, declaring the Church would be filled with God's prophetic anointing to convey and demonstrate God's will and power in all the earth. The Church will be partnering with the Holy Spirit in the end-time scenario.

Joel's promise of an outpouring of the Spirit was partially fulfilled two thousand years ago, and is continuing to be fulfilled today, every time anyone experiences the baptism in the Holy Spirit. Scrutinize the prophetic word of Joel more closely, however, and realize Joel 2:30-32 has yet to be fulfilled. This speaks of a time God will use the Church to release signs, wonders, and judgments upon the earth, resulting in the greatest harvest of souls yet to be saved. Massive deliverances and demonstrations of God's miraculous power are still reserved for, and are taking place in, your lifetime and mine (Joel 2:30-32, Acts 2:19-21).

Therefore, we must contend for and pursue all God's promises to the Church, the Spirit's work, His ministry among us, in us, and through us. Let's stand in faith, believing the greatest outpouring the world will ever see is yet to come, and is even beginning to be released today.

> "Let us know, Let us pursue the knowledge of the Lord. His going forth is established as the morning; He will come to us like the rain, like the latter and former rain to the earth."
>
> *—Hosea 6:3*

> "Ask the Lord for rain in the time of the latter rain. The Lord will make flashing clouds; He will give them showers of rain, Grass in the field for everyone."
>
> *—Zechariah 10:1*

THE POWER OF INTERCESSION
THE SECOND PROPHETIC ACTION IN WHICH THE LORD DESIRES FOR THE CHURCH TO FULLY ENGAGE IS THE MINISTRY OF INTERCESSION.

God's encounter caused me to seriously search my heart. I began to inquire of Him how I could become a vessel prepared, ready to participate in whatever God planned to perform through His Church. I remember lying prostrate, weeping, wondering, "Why am I not prepared? How can I become a vessel, fit for the Master's use?"

I lay there and cried out to God in desperation, "Lord show me how to get ready!"

At that moment, God viewed me as one neither ready for the hour of difficulty nor for the hour of His power. I could not bear it. Over a period of time, and through a series of circumstances, God's Spirit mercifully began to teach me how to prepare myself to become a ready servant.

One of the first areas He highlighted was prayer and intercession. I was already aware of the importance of a private prayer life, but I truly believed intercession required a special calling and anointing, resulting in a deep desire to engage in such ministry. However, as the Holy Spirit began to teach me, I became increasingly convinced of the urgent necessity for God's people to be continually active in intercession. It is not optional; intercession is vital. It is the means by which God allows redeemed humanity to partner with Him in governing the affairs of man.

God's invitation to us today is much like that given to Daniel, when he was given authority to influence the angelic and demonic hosts (Daniel 10:1-3, 10-14). Like Daniel, our prayers carry potential to shift and move spiritual forces in favor of God's plan and agenda. Coming into agreement with God, we are actually releasing strength and power to angelic beings.

Jesus instructed us to ensure our prayers would be in agreement with the will of God and the prayers of Heaven. He taught His disciples to focus their prayers—praying the Kingdom of God from heaven to earth (Luke 11:2).

In other words, we ask for the activity of Heaven to be exacted on the earth. The question is this: What is the activity and atmosphere of heaven? The book of Revelation tells us there are no tears; there is no sorrow; there is no pain; there is no death (Revelation 21:4). God's absolute reign of righteousness and holiness exists around His throne; it is this holy atmosphere for which we are instructed to pray, that it may affect the habitation in the earth.

When we pray, "Let Your Kingdom come, let Your will be done on earth as it is in Heaven," we are actually inviting God's Kingdom to invade the kingdom of man. We are also granting access to the heavenly hosts of God's angels to move at our bidding, as our prayers come into alignment with God's will and God's Word. Prayers are not mere words of man. It is the Word of the Lord we lift up, we pray, and we ask to be made manifest in our midst. The Word of the Lord actually strengthens the angels, giving them the upper hand against the powers of darkness. When we pray according to God's Word and according to His will, the angels excel in strength and are able to enforce the will of God against the enemies of God's Kingdom (Psalms 105:20-21). In the place of prayer, intercession is simply speaking God's Word back to God. It is agreeing with God's revealed will for our lives, our families, our churches, and cities, requesting God's blessings be upon us.

We have been given the promise. If we call upon God, He will answer us. We simply have to obey the call to prayer. If we obey, God's blessings and peace will fill our land (2 Chronicles 7:13-14). In addition to obedience, we must understand the power of agreement with God.

The kingdom of darkness is full of people in captivity and deception. It is no wonder our cities are filled with wickedness, debauchery, and immorality, simply because men and women, young and old, quickly take the bait of satan and are deceived, wildly expressing the agenda of the wicked one. They may not realize it, but these people have essentially yielded themselves over as slaves to the inclinations of their hearts, being influenced by demonic spirits. Satan and his evil works are capable of wreaking havoc in the earth, through the power of agreement. How much more would we see God's power expressed throughout our land, if we would simply come to the place of agreement with the agenda and the will of Heaven? God is greater than satan, and His power is stronger than anything from the gates of hell. Therefore, we have nothing to fear, but to turn to God, yield to Him, and allow His power to be manifest through us.

Before closing this chapter, I would like to give you a few other key points to understand about releasing God's authority in prayer and intercession:

1. GOD PROMISES TO ANSWER OUR PRAYERS ON HIS TERMS, NOT OURS.

He is Lord, and as Lord of the universe, He has a right to dictate what He deems right for our lives and our society. We cannot, and must not, attempt to come before God on our terms. He is the one who wrote the spiritual playbook. He wrote the rules and tells us how they are to be played. Who are we to say, "I don't agree with this," or, "I don't want to do that?"

47

When we choose to humble ourselves and come to Him on His terms, He promises to answer our prayers.

> "If My people who are called by My name will humble them-selves, and pray and seek My face, and turn from their wicked ways, then I will hear from heaven, and will forgive their sin and heal their land."
>
> —*2 Chronicles 7:14*

2. Our Prayers Affect The Destiny Of Nations.

We have already seen the effects of Daniel's prayers; he was able to shift the spiritual powers in the heavens. Reading the story of Moses, and the way God used him and his brother Aaron to set the people of Israel free from Egypt, we should recognize it was primarily the power of intercession, releasing the Israelites from Egypt, bringing judgment upon the land. You may think, "Now, wait a minute, Carlos, it was God's power released through ten plagues on Egypt, which convinced Pharaoh to let Israel go."

I would reply, "You are right."

However, I must point out the impetus behind the plagues of Egypt: actions of Aaron and Moses in the place of intercession, in agreement with God. In other words, had Aaron and Moses not played out their roles as God's messengers, those judgments would not have been released, and God's people would not have been freed from Egypt. Every time Moses or Aaron would lift up their rods in the air, it was symbolic of their releasing God's word in intercession. Exodus records over and over again, Moses standing before the Lord, lifting his rod over the land of Egypt, releasing judgment plagues on Egypt. The rod symbolizes the word of judgment released through the servant of God in the place of prayer. What a pow-erful revelation this is for intercessors today (Exodus 4:17, 20, 7:9-10, 12, 15, 17, 19-20, 8:5, 16-17, 9:23, 10:13, 14:16, 17:5, 9, Psalms 2:9, 110:2, Revelation 2:27, 12:5, 19:15).

3. OUR PERSISTENT PRAYERS RELEASE PEACE AND HOPE IN TROUBLED TIMES.

Whenever Jesus taught on the end times, He showed His followers the key to overcoming. Prayer-filled life releases victory in the midst of great difficulty. The Holy Spirit is actively releasing revelation about the power of prayer, as well as a burden for intercession, so the Church might be ready, prepared to face all manner of evil about to be unleashed from the kingdom of hell. It is for this reason, Christ tells us, men should always pray and not lose heart. Such an edict, in itself, is a revelation about the importance of prayer. We cannot maintain our peace, our faith, or our confidence in God, apart from a life of prayer. The Christian who does not have a prayer life, is one who is easily driven to despair and filled with fear, whenever circumstances begin to threaten personal security. It is interesting to note that in the context of Jesus' discourse about the end times, He gives wise counsel for sustaining ourselves, maintaining consistent and constant diligence in the place of prayer.

> "Then He spoke a parable to them that men always ought to pray and not lose heart."
>
> —*Luke 18:1*

4. INTERCESSION RELEASES JUSTICE TO OUR CITIES.

The continual fervent prayers of God's people are used by God to bring about justice in the land. The enemy will do everything within his power to distract us from continuously coming before God in intercession and in faith. The enemy discourages us with unbelief and fear and tries to convince us our prayers are worthless and powerless. He tells us we're not seeing the full answer to our prayers. The tempter entices us, "Stop wasting time praying." The enemy lures us, "Take it easy; sit back, and enjoy Christian life, like most believers do."

To the one who has tasted and seen God's goodness, however, such advice is nonsense and diabolical. When one has experienced the faithfulness of God in answered prayer, one is convinced that God always hears and always answers. The prayers of intercessors, during the times mentioned in the book of Revelation, are of utmost importance (Revelation 5:8, 6:1, 8:1-6, 15:1-8, 16:1). It will require a strong spirit of faith and persistence to remain faithful to God. Unrelenting prayers continuously oppose the agenda of hell, by standing in faith, regardless of what our eyes and ears see and hear in this natural world. The world may be falling apart all around us, but those who cry out in faith are seeing another Kingdom and another agenda, soon to come upon the earth. Intercessors, in the coming days, will be convinced their prayers are about to be fully answered, and the result will be the reign of justice upon the whole earth, as Jesus comes to establish His Kingdom.

> "And shall God not avenge His own elect who cry out day
> and night to Him, though He bears long with them?"
>
> —*Luke 18:7*

5. Before God's Eyes, Our Identity Is To Be His House Of Prayer.

Clearly, the Church has been deceived and literally deprived of her rightful identity before God. Both the prophet Isaiah, and Jesus Himself, cried out for God's people to be called God's house of prayer. We do everything else but pray, in comparison to the amount of time we spend on evangelism, outreach, discipleship, and all sorts of other church programs and activities. I am not saying we should not be doing all these other activities, but to me, it is quite clear the success in all forms of outreach and church ministries must be rooted and grounded in prayer. If not, we will simply become distracted and serve the ministry as our lord and not serve the Person of Christ. Christian leaders focus so much more time and energy in planning, strategizing, and organizing their ministries than they do engaging in the place of prayer. Pastors and ministry leaders today must return to their places as priests before the Lord and teach their people and congregations once again to come before God and seek His face as a corporate Body. In the next chapter, I want to focus primarily on this point.

> "Even them I will bring to My holy mountain, And make
> them joyful in My house of prayer. Their burnt offerings and
> their sacrifices will be accepted on My altar; For My house
> shall be called a house of prayer for all nations."
>
> —*Isaiah 56:7*

"While I was a full-time student, at the University of Florida, I heard an invitation from the Lord to leave it all behind to build the House of Prayer in Orlando. I decided to give my life to building a house for His Glory to dwell. I would spend day after day gazing upon the beauty of our King. After years of drawing near to Jesus, I received multiple visions and encounters with the Heart of Jesus toward people. He desires to release the power of His Spirit through me to demonstrate His Kingdom of love and compassion for people. The more I fall in love with Jesus, it seems my heart falls more in love with the lost. I realized when I said yes to a life as an Intercessory Missionary, I really said yes to a life of evangelism. He revealed more of my call to me! As it is impossible to draw close to Jesus and not hear the very heartbeat of our Shepherd, I believe out of the prayer movement will come the Gospel to the ends of the earth, manifesting the Kingdom of God!"

—Enrique Gomez Intercessory Missionary
Orlando House of Prayer

"My heart posture is that 'things are not okay right now! The hour is urgent! The time is now!' My mindset must be shaken, as I continue this journey of pursuing Jesus. I want to live my life knowing I did all He asked of me. The song I sing is out of this very place! As I worship, I want my songs to portray complete surrender, manifesting His Kingdom on the earth—not my kingdom, but His Kingdom!

He is moving to raise up singers and worshipers who will sing from a place of desperation and longing for Heaven on earth!

Over the years I've been sitting, singing, and gazing at the beauty of Jesus. He has shown me His Bride being prepared—prepared to manifest His Kingdom with the greatest power of Love!"

—Joanne Gomez Intercessory Missionary
Orlando House of Prayer

Chapter Four

Our True Corporate Identity Before God

Throughout Church history, the Holy Spirit has always moved upon individuals or groups of people to declare God's prophetic will for their generation. When the Church gets desperate enough, God's Spirit begins to draw us to the heart of the Father, for the purpose of receiving His burden and the passion of His heart. The Holy Spirit, consequently, encounters His prophetic servants, so they may reveal His will and the deep, hidden mysteries of God (Amos 3:7; 1 Corinthians 2:9-10).

WHY YOUR CITY NEEDS THE HOUSE OF PRAYER

Once the Spirit opens the eyes of the Church to the will of God, we become enabled to walk in the fullness of revelation, releasing His power and fresh, new levels of the glory of God. These revelations equip the Church to become the witness to the present-day generation, carrying to them the message of the light of Truth.

> "That the God of our Lord Jesus Christ, the Father of glory, may give to you the spirit of wisdom and revelation in the knowledge of Him, the eyes of your understanding being enlightened; that you may know what is the hope of His calling, what are the riches of the glory of His inheritance in the saints, and what is the exceeding greatness of His power toward us who believe, according to the working of His mighty power."
>
> —*Ephesians 1:17-19*

THE REVELATION OF OUR IDENTITY AS PRIESTLY PEOPLE

A major evil in our midst today is the failure to know this God we claim to believe and serve. Countless numbers of folks in the Church are distracted with personal affairs, careers, pleasures of life, or "busy-ness" for God, engaging in "church activities." Being a God of relationship, our Savior desires for us to encounter His love and His presence on a continual, regular basis. Our ability to know God intimately is directly linked to our willingness to come into His presence, which is eternally available to every individual believer. We have the right of access, because of the grace He has extended to each of us (Hebrews 4:16). However, so many do not understand the love of God or grasp the availability of the power of His grace toward us. Distractions of life take hold, and people simply become disinterested or too busy to encounter God, much less to discover how He feels about us. This results in being overly busy in everyday affairs of life, focused predominantly on the temporal life, rather than eternal life and its rewards awaiting those living in dedication and faithfulness to God's Kingdom (2 Corinthians 4:8).

Clearly in Scripture, we are told, before God and before His throne, His purpose is for us to walk faithfully in our priestly identity and authority He has provided. Our priestly anointing carries with it two key expressions, enabling us to fulfill our ministry to the Lord and for the Lord. As priests, we are called to draw near to His presence, by faithfully ministering to Him with our praises and our worship. As we fulfill this expression of ministry to the Lord, the Holy Spirit begins to release the spirit of revelation, exposing to us the heart and will of God and of Heaven for the nations of the earth. This, in turn, enables us to be faithful in the ministry of prayer on behalf of others. God's Spirit begins to release His burden in us, so we might pray effectively, according to His revealed will. We can, therefore, say as His priests, we are, first and foremost, lovers of God. Through our praises and worship, we are also intercessors, as we seek the will of God in the ministry of prayer on behalf of others.

> "Now take Aaron your brother, and his sons with him, from among the children of Israel, that he may minister to Me as priest, Aaron and Aaron's sons: Nadab, Abihu, Eleazar, and Ithamar."
>
> —*Exodus 28:5*

> "They were ministering with music before the dwelling place of the tabernacle of meeting, until Solomon had built the house of the Lord in Jerusalem, and they served in their office according to their order."
>
> —*1 Chronicles 6:32*

> "And has made us kings and priests to His God and Father, to Him be glory and dominion forever and ever. Amen."
>
> —*Revelation 1:6*

Unfortunately, today, though, there are massive numbers carrying out full-time ministry duties within the Church, without intimate contact with the Lord they preach to others. Likewise, the majority of believers, called to serve the Lord in the marketplace, rarely, if ever, connect their hearts in deep fellowship with the Lord, in His presence. Lack of genuine fellowship with the Godhead causes many believers either to develop complacency about their faith, or to become overly active in religious works, apart from a true, intimate walk with the Lord. Of course, the Lord is fully aware of duties we are supposedly performing for Him in His name. The truth of the matter is, however, activity for Him may actually hinder us from knowing or encountering God. It is for this reason, once again, the Holy Spirit is stirring the Church to return to her first Love and to fall in love with her God.

> "I know your works, your labor, your patience, and that you cannot bear those who are evil. And you have tested those who say they are apostles and are not, and have found them liars; and you have persevered and have patience, and have labored for My name's sake and have not become weary. Nevertheless I have this against you, that you have left your first love."
>
> —*Revelation 2:2-4*

This is the most prominent prophetic work of the Holy Spirit in the Church today. He is provoking the Church to once again desire the Lord, as a Bride longs for her Bridegroom Lover (Matthew 9:15, Genesis 3:16). God desires to have a people who will utterly abandon themselves unto Him and His divine purposes for this hour. The strength and foundation of all work to be completed for God must come from a heart of love and adoration. Nothing fuels a heart more than passion, and this passion must be rooted and grounded with a burning love for God, just as He burns and yearns for us (Matthew 9:15, John 2:17). Simply put, the believer who learns to develop in the love of God, one who walks in the first and great commandment, is a believer who will be effective in the ministry of prayer and intercession. It is the love for God that will automatically produce a love for humanity (Matthew 22:37-40). God takes His burden and puts it in our hearts, so we might see what He sees and feel what He feels (Amos 3:7, Nahum 1:12, Habakkuk 1:1-3).

OUR IDENTITY AS A HOUSE OF PRAYER

This book intends to clearly illuminate, in this prophetic hour, one of the greatest truths God is restoring to the Church today: an ability to walk out the first commandment, wholeheartedly loving God. In this season, He is overwhelmingly revealing the Church's bridal identity—as the companion set apart by the Father, for His Son, Jesus. Intimately apprehending the love of God is imperative, so the Church may possess confident endurance to fulfill all other prophetic agendas from God; subsequently, she might effectively manifest the will of God in the earth. This is primarily accomplished through her love (worship) for God and her love (intercession) for humanity. Our restoration as the Bride of Christ will result in our reinstatement into our calling on behalf of the people of the earth, becoming God's house of prayer. The prophet Isaiah, in Isaiah 56:7, prophesied a day in which the Church of Jesus Christ would walk in the fullness of her calling, as the house of prayer for all nations. We must understand what our primary calling is not: Our calling is not to engage in vast building projects, or to accumulate masses of people, nor to conduct great religious services. Neither are we meant to simply serve God, executing religious duties in our faith, without a deep, intimate, personal relationship with Him. We have been called and anointed to draw near to His presence, to encounter His love first and always, so we might be enabled to stand, with courage and assurance, as His representatives on the earth, in the place of intercession. Urgency of this revelation can clearly be seen in the story of Jesus entering into the temple on various occasions, during His final week in Jerusalem. Three main points reveal the seriousness of this matter, before the Lord:

1. Jesus INSPECTS Our Works.

> "And Jesus went into Jerusalem and into the temple. So when
> He had looked around at all things, as the hour was already
> late, He went out to Bethany with the twelve."
>
> —*Mark 11:11*

Just prior to Jesus' betrayal and crucifixion, Jesus makes a final visit to Jerusalem, where He gives us a powerful revelation of the calling on His people, this side of eternity. As He enters the temple with His twelve disciples, Jesus decides to watch and survey the diverse activities taking place in the temple. The temple, we know, according to the Old Testament, was the place where God promised His presence would abide, and His people were invited to meet with Him there. It represented the assurance of God's people, Israel, selected and set apart as His own chosen people from all the nations of the earth. The temple symbolized God's acceptance and God's protection of His people, as long as they walked in obedience to His word.

Choosing not to speak, Jesus simply stood in the temple and observed people responding to the call of God upon their lives. The hour was already late; therefore, Jesus departed the temple with His disciples and returned to the city of Bethany, where He lodged for the night (Mark 11:1-18). Significance of the story is this: Jesus is ceaselessly conscious of the actions of people who claim to follow Him; but more importantly, Jesus is keenly aware of motivations of the heart. A number of ministers in the temple, instead of attending to worship and prayer as faithful priests, were overly occupied with trivial matters. Distractions caused them to disregard the purpose for their existence.

We too, have been entrusted with His presence, and must, therefore, be faithful to attend to the proper works, to draw near to His presence and bring Him glory. The Holy Spirit is inspecting the work of the Church. Days are now upon us, during which God's Spirit is searching throughout the whole earth, to seek out those willing to have loyal hearts, willing to walk in faithful obedience as His lovers and His intercessors. He is highlighting any hindrances in our hearts, which keep us from responding to His call to go deeper, keep us from encountering His power to transform us and conform us to His image. He's calling us higher in Him, so we might be His faithful ambassadors to all the nations of the earth (Romans 8:29, 2 Corinthians 5:20).

2. JESUS EXPECTS FRUIT FROM OUR WORK.

> "Now the next day, when they had come out from Bethany, He was hungry. And seeing from afar a fig tree having leaves, He went to see if perhaps He would find something on it. When He came to it, He found nothing but leaves, for it was not the season for figs. In response Jesus said to it, 'Let no one eat fruit from you ever again.' And His disciples heard it."
>
> *—Mark 11:12-14*

In Scripture, our lives are symbolized as trees, called to bear fruit for God and His Kingdom (Psalms 1:3, Matthew 8:24, Luke 3:8-9, John 15:1-8). If we become trees, planted in God's house, in His word, and in His presence, our lives will truly produce fruit, causing others to taste spiritual truths from God's Spirit, hidden deeply inside our hearts. Each of us is producing fruit, either good or bad. In other words, our lives are testimonies, to bring God praise and allow His work to shine through us, or else to make His work of no effect (Matthew 5:16, 7:16-30).

Having spent the night in Bethany, Jesus returns to Jerusalem, making His way back towards the temple. While walking from Bethany, Jesus notices a fig tree off in the distance and decides to investigate for fruit. He is hungry and wishes to partake; however, the fig tree has no fruit, only leaves on its branches. Significance must be clearly understood to recognize why Jesus did what he did next.

The fig tree boasted of leaves, the promise of fruit, but in actuality was fruitless. In Palestine, leaves of a fig appear first, accompanied by a crop of small knobs. These small knobs become like forerunners of the real figs to come. Peasants or any people passing by are allowed to pluck and eat these knobs of fruit, or the knobs will eventually drop off, before the real fig is formed. If, however, the leaves appear unaccompanied by the knobs of fruit, it means the fig tree will produce no fruit that year. The tree is hopeless and fruitless, producing no harvest.

Expecting to have enjoyed fruit from the fig tree, Jesus pronounces a curse on the tree; it is never again to bear fruit. By cursing the fig tree, Jesus uses the illustration of the fruitless fig tree to make a point, as a prophetic drama, acting out a parable (Luke 13:6-9). Similar to, and prior to, Jesus' dramatic parable, Old Testament prophets demonstrated parallel analogies: Jeremiah bought and broke a clay bottle (Jeremiah 19); Ezekiel made and burned up a model of Jerusalem (Ezekiel 4-5); the Prophet Isaiah removed his prophetic garments to walk barefoot and naked (without his prophetic garment) to prophetically dramatize the coming captivity of Egypt and Ethiopia by the king of Assyria (Isaiah 20). A New Testament example is found in Acts 21:10-11.

We know Jesus expects God's people to produce the fruit of righteousness, and unproductive branches will be thrown into the fire (Matthew 7:16-20; 12:33; 13:4-9, 18-23; John 15:1-8). Thus, the drying up of the fig tree is an acted-out warning.

Proverbs 27:18 displays this truth:

"He who tends a fig tree will eat his fruit, and he who serves his master will be honored."

Jesus' action toward the fig tree teaches His followers what it means to serve their Master, God: simply to have the kind of fruit coming from God (v. 22), or they will wither away if they don't. Jesus neither acts from offense nor performs out-of-character miracles like a magician. Every one of His supernatural acts has spiritual significance. When His Church does not walk faithfully in His call, she is in danger of becoming just like the fig tree. She may look good from the outside but will have no supernatural nourishment necessary to feed others. The key to producing much fruit in our lives is to abide in Him, for without Him, we can do nothing (John 15:5).

"He also spoke this parable: 'A certain man had a fig tree planted in his vineyard, and he came seeking fruit on it and found none. Then he said to the keeper of his vineyard, 'Look, for three years I have come seeking fruit on this fig tree and found none. Cut it down; why does it use up the ground?' But he answered and said to him, 'Sir, let it alone this year also, until I dig around it and fertilize it. And if it bears fruit, well. But if not, after that you can cut it down.'"

Luke 13:6-9

"I found Israel like grapes in the wilderness; I saw your fathers the first fruits on the fig tree in its first season. But they went to Baal Peor, and separated themselves to that shame; they became an abomination like the thing they loved . . . Ephraim is stricken, their root is dried up; they shall bear no fruit. Yes, were they to bear children, I would kill the darlings of their womb."

—Hosea 9:10, 16

3. JESUS CORRECTS HIS PEOPLE TO PRODUCE FRUIT.

"So they came to Jerusalem. Then Jesus went into the temple and began to drive out those who bought and sold in the temple, and overturned the tables of the moneychangers and the seats of those who sold doves. And He would not allow anyone to carry wares through the temple. Then He taught, saying to them, 'Is it not written, "My house shall be called a house of prayer for all nations?" But you have made it a den of thieves.'"

—Mark 11:15-17

Following the fig tree incident, Jesus makes His way back to the temple in Jerusalem. The day before, when He had entered the temple, He had simply examined the activity in God's house. Without saying a word, He held His peace, turned around, and made His way back to Bethany. This time in the temple, however, He no longer observed in silence.

With righteous indignation and a holy anger aroused in Him, Jesus made His way to the tables of the moneychangers and the seats of those who sold doves. He violently overturned the tables and forcefully drove out those engaging in the sale of merchandise.

He boldly declared, to the Jewish Church and religious leaders of His day, the purpose of the temple was not to conduct business nor make profit from the people. His Father's house was meant to be a place of prayer for all the nations of the earth.

How sad it is today, as well, when we become so easily distracted from walking in the eternal identity God has provided and the mandate He has given His people, the Church. Regretfully, we so readily engage in the affairs of life, actually hindering ourselves from living triumphantly in His purpose. Like the Jewish Church in Jesus' day, we have been deprived. We have selfishly utilized the anointing upon our lives to build for ourselves a weak version of Christianity. We have replaced the mandates of worship and intercession, and have made God's house a den of thieves. We have allowed the enemy to steal from us our God-given inheritance to stand before Him, ministering to Him, being strengthened by Him to stand before the people, to minister to them with the authority of the King of the universe. What a privilege and honor He has bestowed upon us, giving us freedom and liberty to boldly come into His presence at any given time, whenever we desire to do so (Hebrews 4:16).

We must, therefore, allow the Holy Spirit to restore the Church today to walk in the fullness of her eternal identity. God calls us and identifies us as His house of prayer. We must not make the Church about building programs or flurries of activity to simulate our Father's business. The business of the Father is walking in our true identity in Him. The greatest privilege in the universe is to dwell in the place of worship, as a lover of God, and to stand before Him and the nations of the earth, as an intercessor. In this hour, God is purifying His Church, to live in Him, to walk in His predestined plan. As we allow ourselves to yield to the dealings of the Holy Spirit, we will have the greatest demonstration of God's power break forth, strengthening us to bring in the greatest harvest the earth has ever seen. The praises of God will resound throughout the earth, as even our sons and daughters are swept into the Kingdom of God, releasing a worldwide outpouring of revival (Matthew 21:12-16).

"*I can imagine when Jesus, in Matthew 21:13, said, 'My House shall be called a house of prayer . . .' He wasn't speaking from frustrated fury, but a place of intimate desire to reveal the glories to His people who value this reality! Jesus was declaring the mysteries the prophets were prophesying! As an intercessory missionary family with two sons, being in the house of prayer with no "how-to-live-this-lifestyle" manuals has had it challenges, but staying the course, going on eight years, we've identified with the Scripture Jesus was quoting from the Prophet Isaiah: 'These I will bring to my holy mountain, and make them joyful in my house of prayer; their burnt offerings and their sacrifices will be accepted on my altar; for my house shall be called a house of prayer for all peoples.' (Isaiah56:7, ESV).*

God desires to restore regions, societies, and nations through a people who govern through the revelation of prayer, worship and intercession! This has been a reality in our family's life. We have seen God bringing justice in the city of Orlando to the unborn through court cases, pro-life legislation, and the placement of Christian political leaders as state representatives. I'M CONVINCED! This didn't just happen, but it has been greatly affected by the praying Church in the state of Florida, contending to exalt Jesus as King, finding joy in His presence, and praying in the Kingdom, as Jesus has instructed His body to do. These words from Jesus are a call (as the prophet Isaiah says) "FOR ALL PEOPLES!" Could it be that Jesus' violent expression in the temple wasn't to condemn, but to open the eyes of His people, almost to say there is more God has for us in ministry than local religious activity? Release the Kingdom, manifesting Gods authority over nations through the house of prayer, bringing healing to many, and allowing His people to exalt Him through song!"

—*Edwin & Heather Botero Full-time Intercessory Missionaries Orlando House of Prayer*

Section Two:

Intimacy With God—"Son, Go Get Your Bride!"

Hearing these words from the Father to the Son caused an array of emotions to flood my soul. I did not know what to think or what to do! In a flash of time, I began to see the passion of God was to prepare the Church to be the Bride of Christ. How blind I had been to this. I had been distracted from this revelation, while I was busy working in ministry. Then the fear of the Lord gripped my heart, as a wonderful reality struck my soul—God desires me!

Chapter 5

Jesus' Revelation Of God As Father

My encounter with the Lord brought with it a major revelation involving Jesus and the Father. Such revelation has had a direct and profound impact upon my heart, a revelation, which could utterly transform us all, if we purpose to intimately know the One True God, the Great I Am. We know Jesus came to die for the sins of man and to offer salvation to the entire human race. However, the purpose of salvation in the first place is for man to have his relationship with God restored, in intimate communion and eternal fellowship. When questioned by Philip, one of Jesus' own disciples, who wanted to have a revelation of the Father, Jesus replied by saying, "If you have seen Me, you have seen the Father."

In other words, Jesus' purpose in coming was for His followers to come to know God as Father, by coming to know Christ intimately, as the Son of God (John 14:7-9).

This is why the Apostle John, writing in his epistle, declares this (paraphrased): "All who would receive Christ as Savior would be given the power, or the right, to become a child of God, simply by believing on His name." This implies the necessity for one to be born of God, by the work of the Holy Spirit (John 3:5-8). It is not something we have power to do on our own; therefore, one must be awakened to this truth:

Only through the Son of God can we become sons of God.

Once our spiritual eyes are opened to our own need of salvation, our eyes are opened to see Jesus as the Son of God—He is the exact image of the Father: full of grace, compassion, and truth (John 1:14).

As we come to know the Son more intimately during our walk of salvation, Jesus, through the Holy Spirit, begins to reveal to us our Heavenly Father. There is a complete misconception in the lives of many believers, which has caused countless numbers to claim only Jesus is full of love, while God is angry about lost humanity and sits on His throne in Heaven, ready to punish the world. Some interpret God only from the Old Testament, and interpret Jesus as portrayed in the New Testament. On the contrary, we must interpret both the Father and the Son throughout the entire revelation of Scripture. Therefore, because the Bible reveals Jesus as the express image of the Person of God, we must conclude, Jesus is just like God, the Father. Jesus does more than resemble God; He is an exact representation.

> "And The Word became flesh and dwelt among us, and we beheld His glory, the glory as of the only begotten of the Father, full of grace and truth."
>
> *—John 1:14*

> "God, who at various times and in various ways spoke in time past to the fathers by the prophets, has in these last days spoken to us by His Son, whom He has appointed heir of all things, through whom also He made the worlds; who being the brightness of His glory and the express image of His Person, and upholding all things by the word of His power, when He had by Himself purged our sins, sat down at the right hand of the Majesty on high, having become so much better than the angels, as He has by inheritance obtained a more excellent name than they. For to which of the angels did He ever say: 'You are My Son, today I have begotten You?' And again: 'I will be to Him a Father', and 'He shall be to Me a Son?'"
>
> *—Hebrews 1:1-5*

From the beginning, God has had a Father's heart. There was a yearning in the Father to have a family, who would choose of their own volition, to come into relationship with Him by accepting Him through His Son. God may be known in Scripture as the Creator and King of the universe, but even the Old Testament reveals Him to be, above all, a Father.

"For unto us a Child is born, unto us a Son is given; And the government will be upon His shoulder. And His name will be called Wonderful, Counselor, Mighty God, Everlasting Father, Prince of Peace."

—Isaiah 9:6

Moses, who is credited with writing the book of Genesis, records the genealogy of man, specifically that of Adam. In Genesis 5, we discover Adam was created in the likeness of God, which means Adam had a resemblance to God. This is confirmed in Genesis 1:27, where the Trinity is recorded as revealing, "Man was made in the image and likeness of God." This bears testimony to the Father's heart, desiring to create man, unlike one of the animals or other created things, rather, creating man like Himself. What Adam was meant to be to creation, Jesus came to restore, so mankind might envision a perfect image of God, with the opportunity to walk in right relationship with God. We are told in Luke's Gospel, although in his fallen state, nonetheless, Adam was considered to be God's son.

"The son of Enosh, the son of Seth, the son of Adam, the son of God."

—Luke 3:38

Jesus reveals many facets of God's personality and nature, but without a doubt, the Fatherhood of God dominates the revelation of Jesus to His disciples, as God's true nature. The English word for *Father* appears 248 times in the Gospels alone, with Jesus addressing God as His Father, in many of those Scriptures. Over half of the references to the word *Father* appear in the Gospel of John alone. Is it any wonder then, one of Jesus' main purposes in coming was to reveal God as a Father to mankind? His constant reference to God as His Father sparked a desire in the hearts of those who heard Him teach about who God really is.

The following verses are but a few references in which Jesus interacted with and communicated His Father before His disciples, the religious leaders, and the common people:

- OUR RIGHTEOUS LIFESTYLE GLORIFIES THE FATHER IN HEAVEN (MATTHEW 5:16).

- THE FATHER WILL REWARD THOSE WHO SEEK HIM IN SECRET, AS WE GIVE, PRAY, AND FAST (MATTHEW 6:1-18).

- GOD, AS FATHER, IS VERY MUCH AWARE OF HIS CHILDREN'S NEEDS FOR PROVISION (MATTHEW 6:26-33).

- JESUS PRAISES HIS FATHER, REVEALING HIS TEACHINGS TO THE HUMBLE (MATTHEW 11:25-27).

- HE CONFIRMS THOSE WHO DO THE WILL OF THE FATHER AS PART OF THE FAMILY OF GOD (MATTHEW 12:50).

- HE ASSURES HIS FOLLOWERS OF THEIR ENTRANCE INTO THE KINGDOM OF HIS FATHER AT THE END OF TIME (MATTHEW 13:43).

- HE CRIES OUT TO HIS FATHER IN THE GARDEN OF GETHSEMANE DURING HIS HOUR OF TRIAL (MARK 14:32-39).

- HE REJOICES AND THANKS HIS FATHER FOR ANOINTING HIS DISCIPLES WITH POWER FROM THE HOLY SPIRIT AND WITH REVELATION OF THEIR SALVATION (LUKE 10:19-22).

- HE TEACHES HIS DISCIPLES TO ADDRESS GOD IN PRAYER, AS FATHER (LUKE 11:1-2).

- HE ASSURES HIS DISCIPLES OF THE FATHER'S WILLINGNESS TO GIVE THEM THE HOLY SPIRIT (LUKE 11:13).

- HE PRAYED TO HIS FATHER, AS HE HUNG ON THE CROSS, ASKING FOR GOD TO FORGIVE THEM IN THE PRESENCE OF ALL (LUKE 23:34).

- HE CRIES OUT WITH A LOUD VOICE AND RELEASES HIMSELF INTO THE FATHER'S HAND WITH HIS LAST BREATH OF LIFE (LUKE 23:46).

- AFTER HIS RESURRECTION, HE TELLS HIS DISCIPLES TO EXPECT FROM HIS FATHER THE PROMISE OF THE HOLY SPIRIT, AND HIS POWER TO COME UPON THEM (LUKE 24:49).

- HE REVEALS THE FATHER IS TO BE WORSHIPPED IN SPIRIT AND TRUTH (JOHN 4:21-23).

- HE BOLDLY DECLARES HE AND THE FATHER ARE ONE, AND THE WORKS HE DOES, THE FATHER DOES THROUGH HIM (JOHN 5:17-32).

- HE TELLS THE RELIGIOUS LEADERS THE FATHER HONORS HIM (JOHN 8:54).

- HE TEACHES HIS DISCIPLES HOW TO ABIDE IN THE FATHER THROUGH HIM (JOHN 14:6-20).

- HE TELLS HIS DISCIPLES HE LOVES THEM WITH THE SAME LOVE THE FATHER LOVES JESUS (JOHN 15:9).

- JESUS' GREAT HIGH PRIESTLY PRAYER FOR HIS DISCIPLES IS FILLED WITH REQUESTS TO HIS FATHER ABOUT THE MEN THE FATHER GAVE JESUS TO MENTOR AND SEND OUT AS HIS WITNESSES (JOHN 17:1-26).

THE FATHER SUSTAINS US IN OUR HOUR OF TEMPTATION

After we receive Christ as Savior, our enemy seeks to destroy our ability to walk with God in complete confidence, as mature sons and daughters, who enjoy the pleasure of knowing the Father's true emotions for His children. Even when a child of God becomes fully convinced of God's willingness to receive him despite personal weaknesses, satan and his demonic forces seek to trap mankind with lies of shame, guilt, and condemnation.

This is vividly expressed in the temptations the enemy wrought toward Jesus. Following Jesus' water baptism by John the Baptist in the River Jordan, the Holy Spirit led Him into the wilderness. The Father had just confirmed His pleasure of Jesus as His Son, His voice ringing loudly from heaven declaring, "This is my beloved Son in whom I am well pleased" (Matthew 3:17).

Up to this point in Jesus' life, there is no record in the Bible of Jesus having performed any spectacular miracle or having done any kind of great work, yet God, as His Father, declares His pleasure over His Son. Our Heavenly Father values a deeply intimate relationship so much more than our doing great works for Him.

Satan fears a people who are rooted and established in God's love (Ephesians 3:17). The enemy will throw every assault against us and try to cause us to doubt the validity of God's love for us, and especially, to doubt His words spoken over our lives. We notice clearly, he even attempted to cause the very one-and-only, begotten Son of God to doubt His own heavenly identity. Three different times he tempted Jesus to do something to prove He was the Son of God. This is the trick of the enemy. He tries to make us believe we must prove our worthiness before we're acceptable to God. In other words, the enemy would entangle us in a religion of works. Look again at Jesus. After each temptation, Jesus resisted every word of doubt, standing on His Father's word and replying back to satan, "It is written."

This was Jesus saying, "Listen devil, I don't have to do anything to prove My value and worth before God, because My Father's Word is enough" (Matthew 3:17, 4:1-11).

His Father had spoken words of affirmation over Him just days earlier, "This is My Beloved Son, in whom I am well pleased" (Matthew 3:17, Luke 3:22).

In the Body of Christ, we must become confident in the Father's love and acceptance, so we will be able to stand against the wiles of the devil. The enemy taunts the believer who is insecure in his relationship with God, as his Father. Such a one will be susceptible to all kinds of fears and doubts over God's goodness and faithfulness for their lives. This will be especially true when facing hardship and affliction.

Jesus, in the Garden of Gethsemane, sweating great drops of blood, inwardly battling full surrender to the suffering of the Cross, trusted His Father. Tempted to seek an alternative, Jesus cried out to His Father, using an intimate term, calling Him, "Abba" or "Papa." This is a term of endearment, respectful yet very intimate. It was a term commonly used in the streets of Israel, as little children would sit on their father's lap and coo, "Papa." The term itself implies assurance of receiving God's kindness and affection. This is clearly one of the Holy Spirit's roles, as He seeks to convince us of our worth to Father God, so we may long to fully know Him and become like Him. As the Holy Spirit reveals God to us as Abba, Father, it touches the deepest need of the human spirit: walking intimately with God, continually receiving His embrace and acceptance.

> "For you did not receive the spirit of bondage again to fear, but you received the Spirit of adoption by whom we cry out, 'Abba, Father.'"
>
> —*Romans 8:15*

SECURITY IN THE FATHER'S LOVE

Because we live in a broken generation, many of our youth have little to no father involvement in their lives, and they grow up to be insecure, with little affirmation. Without an earthly father's example, they find it very easy to doubt the heavenly Father's love for them. In my early years of ministry, as a young youth pastor, I struggled greatly with shame, guilt, and condemnation before God. One early morning, while praying, I began to seek the Lord. One of the very first words coming out of my mouth was this: "Oh, God, please forgive me and cleanse me."

I distinctly remember the Lord's reply: "Forgive you for what? You just woke up."

As ridiculous as it may sound, the sad fact is, many believers live under the same cloud of unworthiness and a sense of shame in their relationship with God. In that moment, my heart was filled with thoughts of condemnation, of not being good enough for the Lord to use me in ministry for His glory. I lived and settled under that cloud, which brought great heaviness to my mind. During this season of my life, the Lord taught me the importance of receiving His unconditional love and grace. It was paramount for me, so I could accept, by faith, all He had done for me. It was important for my children, because my dependence on God relating to me as my Father became the manner in which I related to my children as their natural father. I will never forget the Lord saying to me, "Carlos, it is important you receive and believe in my unconditional love for you, so you are able to show the same unconditional love to your children. For if your children believe in your love, from a father they see with their own eyes, it will be easier for them to receive the love I have for them, as their Heavenly Father, whom they cannot see with their natural eyes."

That revelation made a great impact on my heart, and from that day forward, with my firstborn son barely two years of age, I made a covenant to regularly and continuously tell my children I love them and to show them fatherly affection. It is something I continue until this very day and will continue to do, until the Lord takes me home.

MANIFESTED, GIVEN, DECLARED, AND RESTORED

Unfortunately, for many, we can never know true intimacy with God, as Father, until we experience brokenness, by the discovery of our own sinfulness and emptiness. This is how the prodigal son was able to encounter the unconditional love of his father. After receiving his father's inheritance and wasting every cent of it, he eventually came to his senses, realizing his life was better off in right relationship with his father. God, in similar ways, allows us to travel our own path, knowing we will suffer much heartache, pain, and sorrow. Yet for many, this is the road eventually paving the way back to the Father's heart (Luke 15:11-24). Jesus came to reveal a Father God, who allows us to go our own way, but He is willing and ready to accept us at our lowest point, in our state of brokenness.

In closing out this chapter, let's look at three key works Jesus came to do, in reference to how we relate with the Father.

FIRST OF ALL, HE CAME TO MANIFEST THE FATHER'S NAME TO HIS DISCIPLES (JOHN 17:6).

The word *manifest* means *to render apparent, declare, and show forth.* As we allow the Holy Spirit to manifest the Father's love in our lives, the shame of our own weakness will be overshadowed by His Grace, as our eyes are opened to see the truth (Revelation 3:18).

Secondly, JESUS CAME AND GAVE HIS FOLLOWERS THE WORD OF THE FATHER'S LOVE AND ACCEPTANCE (JOHN 17:8).

Everything Jesus spoke was actually inspired by the Father's revelation of His Grace and love for humanity (John 1:14). The Father reveals the ability to experience truth and freedom, because God's Word is empowered by the life of His Spirit (John 6:63, 8:32).

Thirdly, JESUS CAME TO DECLARE THE FATHER'S NAME TO HIS DISCIPLES (JOHN 17:26).

By this revelatory declaration, Jesus makes known who God truly is to man. When He first called His disciples to follow Him, they were mere servants. As they grew in their revelation of who Jesus was to them, they became His friends, as He made known to them all God intended for them to know. This eventually led to their knowing God as Father (John 15:15).

Regardless what one endures in life, if we will allow God to have His way with us, He will make sure all things will truly work together for our good, especially to those who love God and understand His calling. We return back to Him, especially when all seems lost and confusing (Romans 8:28). Just as the Son of God Himself relied on the Word of God, so, too, the believer who seeks to know God and His Word intimately becomes strengthened in the inner man. God will be the strength of our hearts and our portion forever (Psalms 73:26). The Holy Spirit of God ministers comfort, assurance, and confidence to our hearts; we belong to Him forever, hidden with Christ, in God (Romans 8:15-17).

"In 2011 I had a dream that sealed God's love for me. In my dream a man who was the most beautiful man I had ever seen invited me to follow him to this building. I felt such a draw to Him—I couldn't stop looking at Him and I was wondering where He was taking me. When we got to the building we walked in and he walked me up to two large, closed double doors. He said, 'I have something for you.'

Then he proceeded to open the doors. As I walked in, I immediately saw the most beautiful room. In the room was a beautiful dining table, decorated like no other dining table I had ever seen. It was filled with the most amazing and decadent foods I had ever seen or smelled. I said to Him, 'You did this for me?'

He said, 'Yes, I did this because I love you and I want to spend time with you just sitting and enjoying each other.'

I knew in my dream it was Jesus Who was that Man. My heart became so soft as I sat at the table looking into His beautiful face and gazing into His eyes. Looking into those eyes with my weak glance . . . offering Him my weak love that He so easily accepted. As we talked and enjoyed the food prepared, I knew He was looking and speaking straight into my heart. I knew He had prepared that table for me, because He had missed spending that intimate time with me, where we could be alone, and I could fix my eyes only on Him, and let Him know how much I loved Him, and how thankful I was for everything He had done for me, and in turn, He let me know how much He loved me. It marked me for life. I now wake early every morning to spend time alone with Him. My desire it to gaze upon His beauty all the days of my life and to love Him the way He loves me."

—Emily Sarmiento Prayer Room Director Orlando House of Prayer

Chapter Six

Jesus' Dream & His Desire For Us

During my encounter with the Lord, I was made keenly aware of a second major revelation connecting us to God relationally. God has whole-hearted love toward humanity—His creation. Furthermore, God is Bridegroom God, and we, His Church, are His Bride. This may sound like a strange concept to a lukewarm Body of Christ, but it is sound doctrine, reiterated throughout both the Old and New Testaments. The Lord always reveals Himself as one who takes interest in His people. He is a God who is approachable.

Disciples of John the Baptist asked Jesus why they and the Pharisees valued so highly the spiritual discipline of fasting and mourning, but His disciples did not. Jesus replied with a profound statement, revealing Himself, for the first time, as Bridegroom God. Rather than agreeing with John's disciples' assertion that His own disciples should be fasting, Jesus describes His followers as being in a season of rejoicing, instead of mourning. As friends (disciples) of Jesus (Bridegroom), they had the privilege of constantly being around Him!

John the Baptist was sent as a forerunner to help prepare the way for Jesus' first-coming—an event marked with redemption, restoration, forgiveness of sin, acceptance from God, and much rejoicing with the Messiah in their midst (Luke 1:13-17). It would, furthermore, present a picture of what awaits us in eternity, when the fastings of numerous months will be replaced with the feasting of joy and gladness (Zechariah 8:19). In order to prepare for His coming, however, there was to be a season of repentance, mourning, and fasting, which John represented in His ministry and message. John had been a voice in the wilderness preparing the way to Jesus, and it was a new prophetic season, a time for the people to rejoice. The God of their salvation was among them.

This was the great privilege of the disciples of the Lord, as they began to receive revelation of who Christ was, and what he came to offer. Even John the Baptist testified of this, when he proclaimed even to his own followers, "The Bridegroom has the Bride, but the friends of the Bridegroom rejoice at His coming" (John 3:29).

In this verse, John was pointing to Christ as the Bridegroom and himself as a friend of the Bridegroom. He even affirmed, although he was a messenger (mouth piece) of repentance (fasting and mourning), yet in his heart, he himself had a greater revelation of gladness and joy, for he knew he also was a friend to the Bridegroom God. John rejoiced simply to hear His voice.

Let's take a step further to say this:

> *A friend who hears His voice becomes the messenger,*
> *thus becoming His voice.*

> " He who has the Bride is the Bridegroom; but the friend of the Bridegroom, who stands and hears Him, rejoices greatly because of the Bridegroom's voice. Therefore this joy of mine is fulfilled."
>
> *—John 3:29*

We long to know Him intimately as the Bridegroom God, but in our pursuit, we discover His pursuit of us, His desire to burn away everything hindering love. In the secret place, face-to-face and heart-to-heart with Him, we are transformed, from glory to glory (2 Corinthians 3:18). We become His beloved friend to be made into His messenger.

JESUS TEACHES ON THE KINGDOM OF GOD AS BEING A WEDDING

The Lord Himself taught two parables about the Kingdom of God, within the context of a wedding. In the final week of His life, while in Jerusalem, He was strategic, making sure one of His last teachings was the revelation of an eternal union with God in the eternal Kingdom. In Matthew 22, He compares the Kingdom of Heaven to a certain king or father, arranging a marriage for his son. The king sends invitations to diverse kinds of people to participate in the wedding celebrations. This is a picture of God, the Father, who is sending out invitations to anyone willing to respond, to have a relationship with Him, resulting in our eternal salvation and our perfect union with Him forever. Picturing the Kingdom of God as a wedding, the Holy Spirit, through Jesus, communicates the joy and gladness experienced by redeemed humanity in the presence of our God.

The other key truth to delineate is the necessity of our correct response to the invitation of God. We are to accept His bidding to enter His eternal presence. This occurs only by being attired in the appropriate wedding garment. Just as one dare not attend a very elaborate, costly wedding without proper dress, neither should we expect to be granted entrance into God's wedding for His Son without our hearts being properly dressed. The garment of salvation, through the righteousness and the blood of Jesus Christ and our righteous connection to Him, is what qualifies us to spend eternity with God. Jesus is the only way to eternal life, and all may come freely, to humble themselves and accept His plan of salvation (Deuteronomy 30:6, John 14:6, Revelation 22:17).

> "I will greatly rejoice in the Lord, My soul shall be joyful in my God; For He has clothed me with the garments of salvation, He has covered me with the robe of righteousness, As a Bridegroom decks himself with ornaments, and as a Bride adorns herself with her jewels."
>
> —*Isaiah 61:10*

Jesus' second parable on the Kingdom wedding, found in Matthew 25, declares the need to be in a state of readiness for the actual day of His return. Here, the Lord compares His people: some wise, and others unwise. The wise are pictured as five virgins who have enough oil in their lamps, while foolish virgins are likened to those who have no oil to carry them through the night, should the Bridegroom tarry. Jesus will appear a second time in His nuptial robes, and all His elect, who are prepared for Him, will be beautifully adorned as a bride is for her husband. Those found watching and waiting, with sufficient oil in their lamps, will have the doors opened, to enter into the eternal Kingdom prepared for them.

Unfortunately, the result of the five foolish virgins' lack of preparation was revealed to have caused them to have inadequate supply of oil for their lamps. As a result, they were not ready for the arrival of the Bridegroom. Just like these foolish virgins, the ones who profess to be believers in Christ, but do not have the lamp of God's Word constantly illuminating their hearts to the truth of God's way, will lack revelation to walk in the paths of righteousness (Psalm 119:105). Without the Word of God leading, it is impossible to encounter the level of freedom available to every believer (John 8:31-32).

The wise virgins prepared themselves for the Bridegroom's appearance by making sure their lamps had sufficient oil to burn through the night. It is only by the Holy Spirit (oil) that God anoints our heart to receive the illuminating truths, the joy of freedom in our lives. As we burn, we not only encounter the written Word, but also the Person of the Word in Jesus, our Bridegroom God. The Holy Spirit makes Jesus real, anointing us with truth, causing our hearts to be sanctified and set apart for His glory (Exodus 30:25-30, 1 John 2:20, 27).

Jesus Sends His Forerunners To Prepare Us

The Bridegroom's delay in returning has caused many to slumber and to cease looking attentively for His return. Because His heart so yearns for us, He desires for us to be prepared with the proper spiritual attire, in order for Him to receive us unto Himself. Jesus sends His forerunners, who are His friends, to announce His impending return. John the Baptist is the model forerunner, anointed by the Holy Spirit, to testify of Jesus' appearance, appealing with the Jewish Church to prepare herself.

Modern-day friends of the Bridegroom have the same burning, fiery passion John had, for the sole purpose of ensuring readiness of the Bride and her companions, for the Bridegroom's appearance. They cry aloud: "Behold, the Bridegroom is coming, go out to meet Him."

They have no desire to take attention away from the Bridegroom, but simply to point to Him and give Him all the attention and all the glory. These are faithful servants with prophetic anointing, those who are trustworthy and found faithful before the Bridegroom (John 3:27-31). As others heed the message of these forerunners, friends of the Bridegroom, many will arise from their slumber and properly respond by trimming (*to cleanly burn*) their lamps. The urgent message and righteous lives of these messengers will provoke numerous others' hearts to be set ablaze.

We deceive ourselves into thinking we can serve the Lord with our outer works of service, while neglecting the graces of God's Spirit. It's by His Spirit our bright lamps burn profusely, releasing the fragrance of Jesus' presence and love for all humanity. Holiness and the proper revelation of Jesus, released through the message of His forerunners, will assist others greatly to prepare their lives for His return. Myriads of others will become blazing, forerunner friends themselves. On the other hand, the sad fact remains: Like the five foolish virgins, many will not be prepared in the day of His return, and with weeping and mourning, they will find themselves outside the wedding feast, with the door closed, forbidding them an entrance.

THE JOY OF HIS SUFFERING

The book of Hebrews reveals Jesus as anointed with the oil of gladness, above all others who have ever lived (Hebrews 1:9). This is a profound revelation into the heart of the Lord, as we see the true driving force behind His willingness to suffer at the Cross. It was for the joy set before Him, which gave Him the grace to endure the shame of the Cross and the pain afflicted to His body (Hebrews 12:2). Exactly what was that joy? Jesus' joy was in knowing, by yielding Himself to the Father's will in redeeming humanity, He guaranteed Himself eternal union between Himself and His people (Isaiah 61:10, 62:5). The Lord's heart was obviously fixated upon the promise of the Father and His love for His people. He demonstrated this passion in the way He chose to spend the last week of His life in Jerusalem. He chose to spend much time teaching about love consuming His heart (John 15:9). His priestly prayer, on behalf of His disciples, was filled with requests to share His glory and His perfect union with His followers, just as He and His Father enjoyed theirs.

> "Father, I desire that they also whom You gave Me may be with Me where I am, that they may behold My glory which You have given Me; for You loved Me before the foundation of the world. O righteous Father! The world has not known

80

You, but I have known You; and these have known that You
sent Me. And I have declared to them Your name, and will
declare it, that the love with which You loved Me may be in
them, and I in them."

—John 17:24-26

Even during the final minute of His life on the Cross, He sought to give
one last chance to a dying thief. He promised Him that he would be with
Him in paradise that very day (Luke 23:43). With such great love, such powerful passion, even on the Cross, He was looking to rescue one more sinner,
to bring him into the family of God. His last message, recorded in Holy
Scripture, was spoken through the Apostle John in the book of Revelation.
Even there, in chapters 2 and 3, Jesus releases seven messages to the churches,
filled with loving rebuke, exhortation, instruction, comfort, and admonition.
The Church is reminded to return to her first love, repent of any lukewarm-
ness and any sin hindering her from fully abandoning herself to the Lord
and to the purposes of God's Kingdom (Revelation 2-3). The seven letters
are filled with promises and rewards the Lord gives to His people, simply
for hearing and obeying the instruction of the Holy Spirit, impacting the
heart with truth unto transformation, properly qualifying her to be a people
prepared for His return.

THE PREPARATION OF THE BRIDE

Jesus desires for us to stand before Him in confidence, by His work of
purity in us. It is for this reason, therefore, He committed Himself to send
us the Holy Spirit as our Helper in the transformation of our hearts, from
glory to glory, to be conformed to the image of the Lord (Romans 8:26-30, 2
Corinthians 3:17-18, 1 John 3:18).

One such transformation was the Apostle Paul, who was afforded the
privilege of great revelation and understanding into the mysteries of God.
After having been encountered by the Lord on the road to Damascus, Saul
(who later became Paul) was radically touched by the power of God and later
transformed into the Church's greatest apostle (Acts 9). He became consumed—much like the prophet, John the Baptist—with the Person of Christ,
and genuinely longed to know Him more and more deeply and intimately.

This burning desire ultimately led him to seek God on behalf of the Church, that she might come into this divine revelation paradigm, which would lead her to see herself as the Bride of Christ (Ephesians 5:25-29).

This is truly a day in which the prophetic anointing is falling upon individuals throughout the Body of Christ, like John the Baptist, Paul the Apostle, and John the Beloved Apostle of our Lord, who will be greatly used to prepare the Church for the second coming of Christ. They will be His forerunners who will communicate the Word of God faithfully, until the Church is properly dressed in her bridal attire: the garments of righteousness, obedience, humility of Christ, and lovesick abandonment to the Lord. It's time that you, reader, join the army of forerunners, allowing the Holy Spirit to introduce you to the height, the depth, the breadth, and the length of God's love (Ephesians 3:18-19). You, in turn, will love God in ways only He can love through you.

"I have always been one who longed for and valued the genuine. I was raised in a Christian home and attended church most of my life, but I was on a search for an environment where I could grow spiritually. God's extravagant grace led me through the doors of a House of Prayer in Orlando, Florida.

The moment I walked in the doors, I felt the overwhelming presence of God surround me in a tangible way. I could only weep as the sound of instruments and song met together in a harmonic tune to strike the strings of my heart. I didn't know when I walked into the doors of the House of Prayer that I was actually walking into the doors of destiny and purpose.

The Lord sat me at His feet as He began to reveal His beauty to me. God was on a mission to establish me in truth, by renewing my mind and restoring me from the inside out. I soon joined staff to minister unto the Lord and tend His house. The House of Prayer created a culture of intimacy with God. I was blessed to daily glean from the benefit of the Great commandment being held in first place. It was only a matter of time before I was immersed with a revelation that would overflow from my heart and revolutionize my life. The revelation of Jesus, His heart, desires, emotions and ways, is an unmerited gift, and for the first time in my life, I was able to believe it and access it. The House of Prayer was a greenhouse for my spiritual life, as God used it to grow me in character and knowledge, and teach me foundational truths to equip me. Then at the appointed time, the House of Prayer became a launching pad, as the Lord began to release me to share the message that changed my life, the message of intimacy with Christ."

—Amanda Howard Full-time Intercessory Missionary
Orlando House of Prayer

Section Three:
Kingdom Lifestyle–"No! We're Not Ready!"

These words rolled out of my mouth as I stood there and understood, in my present condition, I personally was not ready in my heart to live this life God was demanding of me. He wanted a complete exchange, my life for His, my world for His Kingdom. It dawned on me; we are in a stage of preparation to be a people made ready for His coming!

Chapter Seven

Living By Principles of the Kingdom

I suggest reading Matthew 5 before reading this chapter.

One glimpse into God's heart, and we are privileged to realize what He has for us, as His people; we see His burning passion to make us His Bride, and we experience His invitation for us to walk intimately with Him throughout our entire Christian journey. Ultimately, we know His eternal plan is to make us one with Him (John 17:11-26). The challenge of dwelling in our weak, mortal bodies, however, is the constant pressure of life and temptation of darkness bombarding our minds and souls, attempting to hinder us from fully experiencing the grace of intimate fellowship with God.

How could one walk then with God in unbroken fellowship and continual favor in this life? The answer is quite simple. We must allow His Kingdom lifestyle to become the governing guide of our daily lives. One of the least understood, much less practiced, principles of Christ is His teaching in the Sermon on the Mount. (Matthew 5-7). In this sermon, we learn the foundational principles of God's Kingdom, as well as His intention to govern in authority over all of His creation. In three humble chapters, Matthew reveals the essence of God's heart, and we become aware of the glaring disparity between His values and ours, specifically pertaining to eternal life and purpose for living.

The Sermon on the Mount
utterly contradicts mankind's paradigms of value, success,
enjoyment, and pleasure.

Observing the life of Christ and His apostles, we notice vividly, their lifestyle was governed by the spirit of humility and righteous discipline. Today's lifestyles, even of those who claim to know Him, are often radically opposed to Christ's standards. I am convinced, in order to fully enjoy the pleasure of being with God, one must come through the gate of humility, dying to self. There are no shortcuts into God's presence. We approach according to His revealed will, or we forfeit the benefits of every privilege the Cross of Christ has made available.

Jesus' Sermon on the Mount was an introduction into the path of righteousness, leading to a life of fulfillment for those genuinely seeking to please God. Let's take a brief synopsis of this sermon by breaking it down into its sub-sections. Jesus begins by addressing eight beatitudes, each one promising a reward to those who seek the path of righteousness in humble obedience and love for God.

THE EIGHT BEATITUDES

Let's face it, the world would be a much better place, if we simply lived by the words written in Matthew 5:3-12. Cooperating with the Holy Spirit and His Grace to live out these Beatitudes, we become strengthened and equipped to be effective witnesses in the world, as salt and light. This lifestyle causes the passionate believer to stand completely apart, as a representative of God in this dark, antichrist world. Though to many, this lifestyle seems too radical, in God's Kingdom, it is basic Christianity.

If I may be so bold as to declare, it is impossible to live out biblical Christianity without commitment to the spiritual disciplines of the eight Beatitudes. In fact, the Beatitudes serve as basic introductory principles, guiding us to a walk of perfect obedience, as the Holy Spirit leads. Our pure-hearted goal becomes absolute submission, while we simultaneously apprehend the Grace of God's mercy and forgiveness, whenever we fall short of His righteous standards (Matthew 5:48). The believer walks in intimate communion with God to the degree he has comprehended revelation of the love of God for him personally. Consequently, he will increasingly be led by the Spirit to walk out these Beatitudes, the foundation of the Kingdom of God.

1. Poor In Spirit

Helps us to see our continual need of, and our dependence upon, God in all areas of life.

2. Mourning

Helps us to express our desperation to be conformed to the image of Christ, as well as our constant yearning to sense the nearness of God's presence.

3. Meekness

Helps us to display a servant spirit by wholly surrendering our lives to God, despite any persecution or opposition from others.

4. Hungering and thirsting after RIGHTEOUSNESS

Helps us to feed continually on God's Word and His presence, in our pursuit of righteousness and deeper encounters with God.

5. Mercifulness

Helps us to enjoy God's mercy, as we treat others with a tender spirit when they fail us, attack us, or disappoint us.

6. Pure in heart

Helps us to be confident in our service before God, through the righteousness of Christ, and to walk in purity in our thoughts, words, and motives.

7. Peacemaker

Helps us to bring wholeness, harmony, completeness, and health to relationships where hostility is present. The ultimate relational healing is bringing sinners to Christ.

8. Persecuted for righteousness

Helps to strengthen our hearts to bear the pressures of persecution and opposition God uses to sharpen our Christian character.

SALT AND LIGHT –IMPACTING SOCIETY —MATTHEW 5:13-16

Jesus used two metaphors to describe the impact of the Church living out the Sermon on the Mount: salt and light. As salt, we release flavor and preservation into the world, which allows God to continually extend mercy to those opposing His righteousness and His laws. Our sacrificial life, releasing the savor of salt, is pleasing to the Lord. We continually intercede before the Father, pleading with Him to extend His love to all who are separated from Him. On the other hand, if we choose to reject the path of righteousness, or attempt to please God in our own strength, we must heed God's warning of becoming worthless salt.

As light, we manifest the works of God, in hope of converting the lost, restoring them to God. Jesus reminded His disciples they were to be like lamps, shining forth the revealed truth of God before men. How we choose to live our daily lives in this dark world really does matter. Unless we follow the paths of righteousness for His Name's sake, our light ultimately will be snuffed out. If we choose not to live in pursuit of God's ordained path, the light of our witness, as faithful servants of God, displaying His grace, love, and character will become null and void.

As an example found in Scripture, Jerusalem was a city whose hill was known as the mountain with the temple of the Lord. The children of Israel were meant to be a light to all the nations, because the temple of God and the God of the presence was their perpetual testimony. By rejecting the covenant of God, however, the Israelites forfeited their city (Psalms 99:9, Isaiah 10:32). As in the days of old, the world is looking for a true witness of the sons and daughters of God, becoming salt and light (Romans 8:19).

FULFILLING THE LAW OF GOD — MATTHEW 5:17–20

Except for God Himself, it is impossible to keep God's standards of righteousness. The law itself is holy, impossible to fulfill; however, our relationship with Christ meets the righteous requirements of the law, because Jesus Himself was 100% obedient. Our connection to Him reckons us into

Him, the fulfillment of the law. Hidden with Christ in God, therefore, we can exceed the righteousness of the Pharisees, whose trust was in their own human ability to keep and obey the law of God.

DEALING WITH ANGER (MURDER IN OUR HEARTS) & BROKEN RELATIONSHIPS
— MATTHEW 5:21–26

Jesus is far more concerned with the condition of our hearts than with our mere outward actions. Jesus, in these verses, is not prohibiting all anger, but only its misdirected usage. Offenses and relational issues cannot be avoided, but we are held accountable for the manner in which we respond to them. Unresolved emotional conflict, like jealousy and anger, can lead to greater offenses, such as the sin of murder, as in the case of Cain and his brother Abel (Genesis 4:1-15).

When our hearts are not grounded in God's love and His forgiveness towards others, it is easy to retaliate, hurling our own accusations against those with whom we are offended. Jesus plainly points to the adverse effect on our ability to enjoy a right relationship with God, if we are unwilling to resolve conflict with a brother or sister. This is the source of great dissatisfaction in our Christian experience, because it keeps us at a distance from Him.

DEALING WITH THE ROOT OF ADULTERY IN THE HEART
— MATTHEW 5:27–32

Selecting David as the next King of Israel, the Prophet Samuel declared, "God looks at the heart" of a man, while man looks at the outward appearance (1 Samuel 16:7-13). God judges intentions of the heart, rather than deeds of the flesh, for from the heart, the body follows suit. We can only imagine what these twelve young men, His disciples, were thinking, as the Lord began to deal with the issue of lust in the heart.

They were probably squirming, as they were seated on the side of the mountain, listening to the words of their rabbi, whom they knew to be a holy man of God. The warning is simple: unrestrained passions of the heart cause the eyes to wander, leading to regrettable acts of adultery, fornication, and other perversions (Proverbs 6:23-29). His solution to the problem sounds even more alarming. He advises them, if they are in prison to their fleshly, sinful desires, to gouge out their right eye and cut off their right hand, rather than risk the fires of Gehenna (hell). Jesus was, of course, speaking about our spiritual eyes and hands, not about our physical ones.

In ancient Middle East, the penalty for rebellion was gouging one or both eyes and cutting off one or both hands. Law was a taskmaster. Jesus' hearers were familiar with this societal punishment, as He conveyed the severity of one's heart of rebellion against God. Christ Himself paid the price to redeem man back to God. The way to escape the sinful heart of rebellion is to accept the righteousness of Christ, and thereby, experience the grace of God, which releases in us the desire to obey Him and submit to His leadership.

STAYING TRUE TO YOUR WORD
— MATTHEW 5:33–37

Taking an oath, or swearing to something, was practiced to secure the reliability of a person's words, to form agreement for commerce, or to guarantee a financial transaction. It was a way to say, "You can count on my word." It was such a common thing to swear by God but not follow through on the oath, resulting in robbing God of His reputation. The reality even today is this: If one's intention is evil, he will deem it necessary to support his own words with an oath. The Apostle Paul reminded us to speak the truth in love, thereby growing in spiritual maturity, affecting the entire life. He taught the Ephesians that lying to one another was an offense against the Body itself and to the Holy Spirit (Ephesians 4:15, 25-31).

EXTENDING MERCY TO THOSE AGAINST YOU
— MATTHEW 5:43–48

Rather than seeking vengeance or trying to get even against someone who has injured you, Jesus counsels His followers to go the extra mile and remain compassionate towards them and seek their good, rather than their punishment. Roman law permitted soldiers to request an individual to carry their load for up to a mile. The law of love, as Jesus demonstrated and lived out, showed His disciples to go beyond the legal limit. For God's love knows no boundaries. Oh, how the world could be saved, if we His servants would simply live by the law of Christ. Our poor example, in many cases, causes others not to draw near to God's love. For this reason, the Lord points us to the perfection of His Father.

Regardless of man's hostility against God, the Lord remains merciful towards all of humanity. By making the sunshine and sending rain, even to His enemies, God, as a Father, is giving us a daily reminder of His continual love and mercy, even to those who do not reciprocate the same back to Him. Jesus' life was an expression of the Person of God. He was, therefore, painting a picture for them of a different breed of people, whom God desired as His representatives throughout the earth. Perfected holiness is possible, only through our union with Jesus.

"The Subject of the Kingdom Lifestyle is very dear to my heart and one that has changed my life completely. Although the entire Bible is sufficient for a Kingdom Lifestyle, I believe there is no greater emphasis on Christ-like living, than in our wonderful Savior, Jesus' Sermon on the Mount, teaching the operation of the Kingdom of God.

In these three chapters of Matthew 5, 6 and 7, Jesus illustrates very clearly and directly, the Kingdom lifestyle in which all believers should walk. From the 8-Core Beatitudes, to the warnings of what can take our hearts astray, to the life of fasting and prayer and forgiveness, Jesus outlines incredible life-changing principles to live victoriously through these Kingdom principles.

For me, it really hit home in 2007, when I visited the International House Of Prayer in Kansas City, MO. As I entered the doors of that ministry—strictly as a visitor for a conference—suddenly the head person of their bookstore saw me, and without having ever met me, she rushed and got a whole bunch of teaching material, and put a big pile of these teaching materials in my hands, and it was all for free. On the very top of all these resources, as I looked at the very top title, it said: The Sermon on the Mount! Ever since that day, I have purposed in my heart to study these principles, and in the process of studying them, I have been Encountered by God in a whole new, powerful way. Since then, I've dedicated my life to teach and live out the Sermon on the Mount Kingdom lifestyle! I pray you do the same as I did."

—George Sotolongo
Pastor
Orlando House of Prayer

Chapter Eight

Confident In Who God Says You Are — Matthew 6 & 7

I suggest reading Matthew 6 and 7 before reading this chapter. The mystery of the Kingdom of God is revealed not to the human eye. In other words, the Apostle Paul and Jesus teach us, God's Kingdom first is manifest in the hearts of its citizens, who have chosen to accept Christ as their King. As we yield to His leadership and submit our lives to His Word, the Holy Spirit supernaturally produces the character and life of the Kingdom in the inner man (Luke 17:21, Romans 14:17). When speaking of rewards, it's important to understand, God does not just reward us according to what we do for Him in this life, but according to the pursuit of our wholehearted love and obedience to Him, which aids us in enlarging the Kingdom of God in our hearts.

Giving , Praying , Fasting & Rewards — Matthew 6:1–18

In His teaching in Matthew 6, Jesus describes three main activities, which greatly assist our hearts to receive more of God's grace and strength, as we faithfully and consistently serve Him with our charitable giving, prayers, and our voluntary fasting. These are spiritual disciplines, positioning our hearts before God to receive more of His grace (James 4:6). God rewards us for our sacrifice, not with temporal things, such as popularity, greatness before men, or abundance of earthly riches, but with His presence and a greater measure of His glory upon our lives. The life of Christ in us will become increasingly evident to others, as our lives are impacted by the power of the Resurrected One, and others will see the metamorphic transformation. We can choose to focus our energy, desiring to be seen by men and to be recognized as religious, spiritual followers of God, but that does nothing to guarantee the pleasure or favor of God. Jesus gives us the choice to either be seen by men or to receive our reward from our Heavenly Father, who sees our giving and sacrifice done in secret, for the Father alone to recognize. In essence, men's recognition of us, as a result of our own self-promotion, even for doing some great work, will cause us to already have received our reward. All earthly acknowledgment will fade away as quickly as it came upon us. In contrast, the Father is able to discern the true motive of the heart of the one who solely desires to be seen by God alone. This kind of disposition reaps great rewards in the Kingdom of God.

> ### The whole point here is to encounter God's heart and to have Him encounter and transform ours.

Jesus continues by saying there are some who love to actually come before God in prayer, for the sole purpose of being seen as some great prayer warrior. Again here, Jesus says their desire to be seen and recognized has become their reward. But to the believer whose heart is truly to seek after the revelation of God, hidden in the secret place, that one will be rewarded openly.

Jesus teaches us, one's prayer life need not consist of vain repetitions, in hopes of getting God's attention. The true seeker's reward is actual encounter with God's revelation, to know, more and more deeply, God is his Father, and he is God's child. In other words, God introduces Himself as a God of intimacy and a God who seeks a relationship with His children. What security, what confidence this produces in the life of the true seeker. This newfound liberty in one's relationship with God begins to reveal to us things that hinder our ability to sense the closeness of God's presence. Knowing God intimately also opens our eyes to the strategies of our enemy, only to assure us of victory against all his assaults of darkness.

The Lord's Prayer is a beautiful picture of what prayer can be, when we are assured of God's acceptance, as we learn to surrender our hearts in wholehearted devotion to the Lord. Jesus' teaching on prayer in Matthew 6:9-15 reveals God as our Father, whose name is Holy. He wills for His Kingdom to invade our lives. The same passage discloses the Father's willingness to meet all of our daily needs, as He forgives all of our sins. In order to experience the power of His forgiveness, we also must be willing to forgive others who've offended us. Thus, we will be strengthened in His grace to resist all forms of temptation and the plots of the evil one over our lives. Our lives will be filled with praise and the experience of the power of God.

Jesus continues to teach on fasting, where again, He warns us of the desire to be seen and known by others as religious, disciplined followers of His. This attitude will come at the expense of forfeiting God's grace to truly have our hearts encountered by our Heavenly Father. The fruit of one truly seeking the Lord in spirit and in truth, and for no recognition from man, will be a great confidence to boldly and humbly approach God at any given time, as desired. God's transforming power convinces the heart that God's presence is a safe place for the seeker. The Holy Spirit begins to cleanse the believer from any fear, shame, guilt or condemnation. The Spirit of God eradicates the enemy's tactics with the assurance of forgiveness, of being completely acceptable in the sight of God, through the blood of Christ (Hebrews 4:16).

HEAVENLY TREASURES & EYES OF REVELATION — MATTHEW 6:19–23

Ability to seek and attain treasures in Heaven is in direct proportion to that upon which we choose to set our gaze. If our eyes are given over to seek after the pleasures of life, anything we may attain will eventually be lost. Earthly resources, no matter how much temporal value they may hold, one day will all be worthless. On the other hand, if we choose to pursue spiritual treasures, focusing our eyes upon those things in which God places everlasting value, we assure ourselves of attaining eternal riches, which will never lose their worth throughout all eternity (Ephesians 1:7, 18, 2:7, 3:8, 16).

SERVING THE MASTER & TRUSTING HIM FOR ALL OUR NEEDS — MATTHEW 6:24–35

In this prophetic hour, the Holy Spirit is encountering hearts of individuals in the Church who are just plain tired of mundane "Church-ianity." That's a word I made up to express the lifeless, boring version of Christianity. To me, it is no wonder there is little power or victory in the lives of many Christians today. It's simply because we are serving the wrong master. Many of us have foolishly adopted an unbiblical version of Christianity, which cannot be found in the writings of the apostles or the teachings of our Lord Jesus. To believe we can embrace the modern progressive liberal teachings of the Church today and at the same time claim to serve the Jesus of the New Testament is nothing more than outright deception. Jesus makes it very clear; it is impossible to serve two masters. A master requires 100 percent loyalty of his subjects. Which are we going to serve, the God of the Bible or the god of this world, who uses the enticing riches of life to distract us from the true King of the universe? The meaning of the English term *mammon* is derived from the Aramaic for *riches* meaning *possessions*, as well as *money*. The root of so much fear and worry in life comes from having the wrong allegiance in our hearts to the wrong master (*mammon*). If we really believe Jesus is Lord of our lives, we would relieve ourselves of so much anxiety, keeping us bound to the stuff of this life. Trusting Jesus as Lord means our lives are not filled with worry; our hearts are fixed on the works of His Kingdom, because we know that He has all of our needs in mind. The key to unlocking God's divine provision is to focus upon what the Kingdom of God requires—surrender and trust!

In the last chapter of His Sermon on the Mount, Jesus continues to teach on the deeper truths of the Kingdom of God. He shares the importance of avoiding a critical, judgmental spirit, learning to continue to stand in faith and prayer, and the importance of persevering until God sends a breakthrough. He differentiates between the narrow and wide paths, and He teaches His followers to be able to discern true servants of God from false, by observing the type of fruit they produce from their lives. He warns about the dangers of building our security in God from performance of good works in His name, and He rebukes the individual who builds his house on any foundation other than the Word of God.

BE CAREFUL HOW YOU JUDGE
— MATTHEW 7:1–6

In our pursuit of righteousness, as we seek the Lord in walking out the Kingdom lifestyle described here in Matthew chapters 5-6, we can be assured our relationships with others in the Body of Christ will surely be challenged. The temptation would be for the seeker to become critical of others who pursue God with less intensity. This flings wide the door and opens our hearts to the temptation of hypocritically judging others. We must remember; each of us is being dealt with by God's Spirit in different ways, at different levels, and in different sequence. We must remember; each of us, at one time in our spiritual walk, was embracing things, which today we no longer deem acceptable. Passing judgment upon others, especially the unbeliever, with a critical religious spirit, is equivalent to throwing precious pearls before a pig, without the insight to perceive true value. It is not our job to convince people of their lack of spirituality, using the precious truth of God (Matthew 13:45-46). We are not to hammer them with revelations from God's Word, but we are to pray and allow the Holy Spirit to convict them of sin, to bring repentance, to counsel, and to illuminate truth to them.

ASKING , SEEKING , KNOCKING IN PRAYER
— MATTHEW 7:7–12

Jesus exhorts His followers to keep prayer as a priority, when dealing with all the issues of life. Having taught His disciples to trust God as Father for all of life's necessities, and to remain benevolent, even when relationships are strained and seemingly hostile against us, Jesus encouraged believers to keep asking, seeking and knocking. Our confidence, while being persistent in prayer, demonstrates our trust in a God who is our Father, not an impersonal god. As a Father, He is more than benevolent, willing to hear us when we cry out. He fills our hearts and prayers with faith and confidence in the power of God to answer us and fulfill His promises.

CHOOSING THE NARROW GATES OF LIFE THAT PRODUCE FRUIT
OF RIGHTEOUSNESS
— MATTHEW 7:13–20

Knowing there would be plenty of opportunities to turn back from pursuing the Lord in the way of righteousness, Jesus reminds His followers of the enemy, who will always present to us the wide gate. It's wide, because it is easy to find, and many who reject the disciplines of righteousness will be found there, encouraging others to join them. This seems to be the popular message of the hour in many Christian circles. We are living in a day in which many are choosing not to seek the Lord or His will, but instead are settling for a man-made version of Christianity. This was the warning of the Apostle Paul, when he wrote the Epistle of Jude 1:3; we must contend earnestly for the faith, delivered to the saints of God. Deceivers had been creeping into the Church, turning God's grace into licentiousness, bringing false teachings, claims of Jesus not being Lord or not the only way to God. God's Word is clear. When one becomes a servant of Christ, he becomes a new creature, and God equips him with the power of grace to live a godly life, by turning away from immoral habits, controlling the lives of unbelievers. We must not apologize for the standards of holiness found in the teachings of the Lord Jesus. Our lives are either producing good fruit or bad fruit, and we should be able to discern the life of anyone speaking on behalf of God, by observing the spiritual fruit they are displaying (Galatians 5:19-25).

KNOWN BY GOD BY BUILDING UPON HIS WORD — MATTHEW 7:21–27

Jesus ends His teaching by reminding us of the goal in our lives and of the danger of missing our divine purpose for existence on the earth. There is a day coming when all mankind and the nations of the earth will stand before the Lord—both those in the Church and those outside of the Church. Simply because I believe something as being Christian, doesn't mean God automatically will accept it and see it as such. God and His Word are the standard, not our personal perceptions. Revelation 2 and 3 reveal to us the awareness of God's ability to see things for what they really are. We may look good on the outside to men, but God is able to pierce within the heart of the Church and of the individual—judging in truth and righteousness. The way to secure our lives upon the proper foundation is not to build upon the approval of man or upon the riches this life may offer. By building our lives upon the solid foundation of the Word of God, we allow the Holy Spirit to encounter us, and thereby, transform our lives. He desires us to be a place of habitation for the God of glory to take delight in abiding there. Jesus' words are filled with authority and have the ability to build our lives, so we may bring Him great praise, glory, and honor.

We cannot afford to continue life as it is without allowing the Lord to close the door to areas of our lives that are fruitless, dry, and barren. The Spirit of God is seeking to raise up a different kind of messenger who will embrace the truth of God's Word—communicating it faithfully!

> *Our love and obedience will be tested in order*
> *to prove our genuineness under the pressures of life.*
> *The question each of us will have to answer is this:*
> *"Are we able to endure and remain faithful to the Lord?"*

Time will tell. Jesus Himself will be the only One to have the final word to this question.

"As an intercessory missionary you must have confidence in who you are before the Lord, this was not always the case with me. As a young believer I struggled with my identity. I constantly had to deal with shame, fear of man, and several other insecurities. I knew I was forgiven, I knew there was freedom available but I let myself be controlled by the lies of the enemy. It was in the place of prayer where I found freedom. Imagine a place where constant prayer and worship is being lifted up; it creates the perfect atmosphere to hear the Lord. I would come daily to the house of prayer to seek the Lord and that's where I experienced breakthrough. It was in this place, where I learned how He felt towards me and what His Word says about me.

Then, in that place, I realized my identity isn't based on my past, what I do, or what anyone says about me but it is based on what He says about me. With this revelation my life was changed. I now have confidence to approach Him in prayer. I also grew in the giftings and talents he placed in my life that were often hindered because of fear. Now the Lord can use me freely, and I can approach the throne of grace boldly, knowing He hears me and accepts me."

—*Nick Botero Intercessory Missionary Orlando House of Prayer*

Chapter Nine

How God's Kingdom
Rules In Our Midst Now

There is a great and urgent need to understand biblical teachings about the end times in order for our hearts to be found ready so that we do not become majorly offended at the events that will take place prior to the coming of the Lord. We read in Matthew 16:1-4 that Jesus rebuked and corrected the religious leaders of His time for not discerning the signs of the times which pointed to His first coming. In Luke 12 Jesus addressed the common people of His day and rebuked them for not being alert or discerning the spiritual events that were being fulfilled in their day. We endanger ourselves spiritually when we ignore the prophetic writings about His second coming and choose to rather embrace the lukewarm and complacent gospel that is being preached to us on a weekly basis behind the pulpits of our churches in America.

When the Pharisees approached Jesus, they asked Him when the Kingdom of God would come. Jesus answered them saying, *"The Kingdom of God does not come with observation."* In other words, Jesus was saying that we should not expect that things will all of a sudden change entirely from one day to the next. It will take more than that for God's Kingdom to be perfectly established and settled upon the earth.

> "Now when He was asked by the Pharisees when the Kingdom of God would come, He answered them and said, 'The Kingdom of God does not come with observation.'"
>
> —*Luke 17:20*

The Lord warned that we must be aware of the deception: *"Look over here or look over there; here is the Kingdom of God."* He knew that false prophets would arise and draw people after themselves and detract them from the Kingdom of God. Knowing that this deception would be upon the earth in the last days, Jesus clarified where the Kingdom of God is and how it would come to the earth. He said, *"The Kingdom of God is within you"* (Luke 17:21).

This is very important to understand because having the Kingdom of God inside of us means that we must learn how to release the benefits and the power of God's Kingdom. We must realize that if there is a kingdom, then that means there is a king that presides over that kingdom. Obviously, the King that the Bible talks about is referring to the Lord Jesus Christ.

If we are going to see the
Kingdom of God come, we must first know that
the Kingdom of God lives in us and flows through us. We must
yield to Jesus' Lordship and allow Him to be both Lord and King,
that He may have dominion over our hearts.

There is such turmoil in the nations of the earth because the Church has not presented the Kingdom of God well, nor have the nations allowed Jesus' leadership to rule over them as the rightful King of the earth. When the Lord is really King, it is then that we will see Jesus not just as the Savior but also as the Lord that will allow for the Kingdom of God to manifest in our midst.

One of the key problems that I see in the Western Church is that we simply want to hear about a nice Jesus who cuddles us; a Jesus who says nice things to us, a Jesus who promises to prosper us and a Jesus who vows to make us successful. The Western Church simply loves the gospel of success and the gospel of prosperity. We live on that! We have become consumed and bent on going after the "American dream," while we shun and despise the true teachings of the Gospel; the Gospel that promises us that if we desire to live a godly life we will suffer persecution (Matthew 5:10-12).

That concept, however, offends us and causes us to resist any such thought or any such teaching. Why would we despise and reject the very thing that Jesus said would guarantee us blessings? We are so comfortable in western society that we picture a gospel that guarantees us certain benefits and promises that are sure to make everything work out perfectly according to our plans. What if God's plans included that some of us were to become martyrs? What if His plans for your life included living in the inner-city all the days of your life, simply because God has a plan to use you to bring revival and to shake up the inner-city where you live and deliver the souls that are in bondage? What if that was God's plan for your life?

A lack of truly understanding what the Kingdom of God really is has caused us to fabricate our own gospel that is more appealing to our lifestyle. So many in the Church have partaken of satan's bait, which lies to us and says that unless we have the latest car model or live in a certain size home we are not really living a successful life. This is not the Gospel! I am not saying that God is asking us to live poor lives but what I am saying is that the same God who called the Prophet Daniel to live in the palace of the King of Babylon is the same God who also called Ezekiel to be a prophet in the slave camps of Babylon among his own countrymen, the Jews. What God may have for you may be totally different than what He has for me. We must not compare our lives to one another and conclude that we must have the same things that others have because we serve the same God. We must understand that God's plans are individually prepared for each and every one of us according to His will. Not properly understanding this principle will eventually cause us to be discontent in our walk with God. This hinders us from being able to have a deep, personal and intimate relationship with Christ. Striving for the things of this natural world snatches the grace from our hearts to desire a life of prayer and a hunger for God's Word; the Word that will both speak to us and nourish us day in and day out. The Church is guilty of going after stuff when the Lord is saying to us, *"Come after Me and I will cause you to hear My voice and to know My will that you may communicate the Kingdom of God to others."*

Oh, to be a voice for God and to be His messenger is what we must long for and contend for in this day and hour of compromise!

The Holy Spirit is looking to anoint prophetic messengers who will loyally represent the Gospel of the Kingdom of God well—in a way deemed worthy of the King of kings and Lord of lords. This is what it means to be prophetic (Revelations 10:8-11)!

SEEKING TRUE REWARDS

My heart truly desires to go after the rewards that are found in God and will be rewarded in all of eternity. There is a grace that the Holy Spirit will impart into the heart of the believer to make us willing to contend for the true riches of the Kingdom of God. I disdain and am disgusted by the thought of seeking to become something great on this side of eternity, when I know from Scripture that God's Kingdom will offer me so much more on the other side of eternity.

> "Whoever therefore breaks one of the least of these commandments, and teaches men so, shall be called least in the Kingdom of Heaven; but whoever does and teaches them, he shall be called great in the Kingdom of Heaven."
>
> *—Matthew 5:19*

> "And behold, I am coming quickly, and My reward is with Me, to give to every one according to his work."
>
> *—Revelation 22:12*

I long and hope to hear those precious words of Jesus that will say to me that I am a good and faithful servant simply because I made the Kingdom of God my desire—for His praise and His glory (Matthew 5:21-23). If the Kingdom of God is truly inside of us then we need to allow the characteristics of that Kingdom to manifest through us. When someone offends us we need to forgive them and when people curse us we need to bless them in response. When people offend us, we need to pray for those people. These are the fruits of God's Kingdom that begin to transform the hearts of those asking the Lord for more of His reign in the midst of their lives (Matthew 5:44). Therefore, let us pursue the Kingdom of God and allow His peace to rule in our hearts and release supernatural joy in the midst of life's trials and tribulations. *What greater reward can one ask for than to have the strength and peace that God's Kingdom deposits within us?*

A GENERATION THAT DESIRES GOD— A KEY CHARACTERISTIC OF THE KINGDOM

Jesus went on to say that there would come a day when the Church would begin to desire one of the days of the Son of Man and that they would not see it (Luke 17:22). As I read that one morning during my devotional reading I felt like the Lord wanted me to dig deeper into this scripture and ask for deeper revelation of what He might be saying to me and to others. I began asking the Lord, *"What were You trying to say to Your disciples? What do You mean that there would be a day coming that they would desire to see You but they wouldn't?"*

I thought to myself, *"If Jesus could say that to His own disciples in a time when they actually walked with Him, saw Him and daily fellowshipped with Him, then couldn't He actually say the same to us today? If He said that to them, how might that apply to us today as well?"*

Jesus said, *"There will come a day,"* and I believe that day is already upon us, *"when the Church as a whole will begin to once again long for the presence of the Lord, similar to what the early disciples had and knew."*

You see Peter, James, and John did not have to desire to see one of the days of the Son of Man because Jesus was already there with them in flesh and blood. This may have applied to them during the time after His crucifixion when they were in deep mourning for Him, being greatly troubled that their Lord had been taken away from them. Eventually, they did see him three days later and during the 40 days after His resurrection. These precious encounters the disciples had with Jesus flooded their hearts with great joy and peace.

> "Then He said to the disciples, 'The days will come when you will desire to see one of the days of the Son of Man, and you will not see it.'"
>
> —*Luke 17:22*

> "A little while, and you will not see Me; and again a little while, and you will see Me, because I go to the Father... Most assuredly, I say to you that you will weep and lament, but

the world will rejoice; and you will be sorrowful, but your sorrow will be turned into joy. . . Therefore you now have sorrow; but I will see you again and your heart will rejoice, and your joy no one will take from you."

—*John 16:16, 20, 22*

I believe the Holy Spirit is awakening the Church to understand and realize that we have been so busy doing all kinds of ministry for hundreds of years but we have done so without the nearness of the presence of Jesus in our midst. We are living in a day when the Spirit of God is once again awakening the Church by imparting bridal affections for Jesus much like a bride who longs to be united with her bridegroom. He is stirring up deep love for the Person of Christ that we may once again experience the nearness of His presence like the early Church did in the days of the apostles. The apostles were successful in their ministry because Jesus was the main emphasis of the ministry. In other words, they did not allow the busyness of ministry to keep them from ministering to and loving the Lord. They walked intimately with Him and sought His presence through prayer, worship and obedience to the Spirit's leading. These are all characteristics of kingdom-minded servants of God (Acts 2:1, 4:13, 24-31, and 6:1-11).

When the Church eventually wakes up to this reality, we will begin to desire and long for the presence of the Lord that has been taken from us because we have been distracted with the needs of the ministry. The emphasis on intimacy with God that is happening worldwide today is a prophetic sign that the Holy Spirit is moving in a fresh and urgent way to restore the Church to her first love. I believe this is the reason why there is a great witness in the nations of the earth with ministries that are popping up worldwide that have a passionate desire for night-and-day prayer mixed with continual praise and worship. How I rejoice to be a part of such a prophetic hour as this.

What the Early Church Knew

What were some of the Kingdom realities the early Church walked in? For one, the disciples were given the privilege of being able to encounter Jesus in the flesh. Christ had dwelt among them and had revealed the glory of the Father to them so they became men and women who were accustomed to the presence of the living Christ. (John 1:14). These disciples were not simply following devised fables or hearsay tales. These were men and women who were willing to give up all and surrender themselves wholly in utter abandonment to the cause of Christ. Why? Because they had encountered Christ in the flesh and they were eyewitnesses to His death, burial and resurrection. These were followers who were communicating and writing out of experience when they said, "We were eye-witnesses" (1 Peter 1:16). They were not following mere rumors or made-up stories, but on the contrary, they were actually physical witnesses of His glory and were invited to see Him, touch Him and follow Him!

> "'Behold My hands and My feet, that it is I Myself. Handle Me and see, for a spirit does not have flesh and bones as you see I have.' When He had said this, He showed them His hands and His feet."
>
> *—Luke 24:39-40*

> "That which was from the beginning, which we have heard, which we have seen with our eyes, which we have looked upon, and our hands have handled, concerning the Word of life—the life was manifested, and we have seen, and bear witness, and declare to you that eternal life which was with the Father and was manifested to us— that which we have seen and heard we declare to you, that you also may have fellowship with us; and truly our fellowship is with the Father and with His Son Jesus Christ. And these things we write to you that your joy may be full."
>
> *—1 John 1:1-4*

A major difference between the early Church and the Church of today is that most in the Body of Christ are only hearing about having encounters with Christ. Rather than being able to have their own testimony of personal encounter with God, they are limited to merely hearing about God encountering other hungry, desperate believers today as He did His first followers. God is no respecter of persons and His ways do not change. He was willing to reveal Himself 2,000 years ago and He is willing to do so today as well. If we would choose to focus more on our relationship with God and pursuing Him rather than the affairs of this life, our hearts would come alive and He, by His Holy Spirit, would begin to manifest Himself to us. We have churches and ministries that emphasize activities, programs and so much busyness that by default we are raising up a passionless and self-absorbed generation that is not capable of hearing from God or encountering Him on a regular basis. This is a travesty when we understand the true purpose of Jesus' ascension and why He said it would be to our benefit that the Holy Spirit be sent to the earth (John 14:16, 15:26, 16:7). Beloved, God's Holy Spirit has been given to us so that we might know Him as the early Church knew Jesus. It is the Spirit of God who seeks to reveal Jesus to us.

> "But as it is written: 'Eye has not seen, nor ear heard, nor have entered into the heart of man the things which God has prepared for those who love Him.' But God has revealed them to us through His Spirit. For the Spirit searches all things, yes, the deep things of God."
>
> —*1 Corinthians 2:9-10*

The Apostle Paul plainly tells us, *"The deep hidden things of God are made known to us by God's Spirit."* We have been given the Holy Spirit so that we might come to know all things that have been freely given to us and are available to us. This bears witness and is in agreement with what Jesus said the Holy Spirit would do when He would come (John 14:26, 16:13-15).

Days to Restore The Great Commandment

The days to seek after the knowledge of God are now upon us. There is a major emphasis by the Holy Spirit to pursue intimacy and love for Jesus as He is stirring up the heart of the Church to awaken us and to help us long for and desire the same "one thing" that consumed David's life (Psalm 27:4).

> "He who has clean hands and a pure heart, who has not lifted up his soul to an idol, nor sworn deceitfully."
>
> —*Psalm 24:4*

"O God, You are my God; Early will I seek You; My soul thirsts for You; My flesh longs for You In a dry and thirsty land Where there is no water. So I have looked for You in the sanctuary, to see Your power and Your glory."

—Psalm 63:1-2

David was known to be a man who was addicted to the presence of God. Nothing else satisfied him to the point that even his flesh craved to encounter God's presence (Psalms 63:1-2). I believe this is what the Church in the end times will look like and be characterized by; a people that can be referred to as the "Bride of Christ," simply because they will be a generation who prioritize the Kingdom of God in their midst by seeking to live out the great commandment of loving God with their entire being (Mark 12:30, Revelation 22:17). This, in essence, will create great turmoil within the Church itself. Many will resist the testimony of those becoming lovesick for their God and will begin to persecute those who truly desire to live abandoned lives for Christ. Much like Ishmael, who persecuted Isaac and Esau and hated Jacob, there will be a great division in the Church, simply because of the remnant that will be arising. This remnant will begin to boldly declare and manifest the Kingdom of God in the earth (Genesis 27:41, Matthew 10:33-35, Galatians 4:22-29).

This manifestation of the Kingdom of God will rub the lukewarm carnal Church in the wrong way and stir her to persecute and betray those in the Church who truly know and love God. In closing this chapter let us understand that when the Kingdom of God is manifesting in the life of a believer it invites the authority and power of the Kingdom to be displayed. This is what will empower the true Church to give herself completely to winning the lost and bringing justice to the nations of the earth. Only when we truly love God with all of our heart will it be possible for us to love our neighbors as ourselves, even unto death.

"And you shall love the Lord your God with all your heart, with all your soul, with all your mind, and with all your strength.' This is the first commandment. And the second, like it, is this: 'You shall love your neighbor as yourself.' There is no other commandment greater than these."

—Mark 12:30-31

111

"By this we know love; because He laid down His life for us. And we also ought to lay down our lives for the brethren."

—*1 John 3:16*

"The signs Jesus shared about His second coming in Matthew 24:3-14 can be seen everywhere. As lawlessness increases in the land and darkness runs rampant, one cannot help but be overcome by a sense of urgency. Having a heart for the inner city and the privilege of working in some of the darkest fields, it is impossible for me to not grasp this hope as my anchor; it is the belief that Jesus' return is so much closer then we can think of. With this comes the expectation that when He finally arrives, all things will be changed for the good. I've witnessed a city whose streets are swarming with homeless youth, whose motels reek with the stench of human trafficking, where homosexuality is paraded around, and where false prophets line the streets, bringing condemnation to the world. How can the Bride of Christ, sharing the heart of the Father, desire anything less than to cry out in intercession for Jesus' return?

I merely have to open my eyes to see that this passage in Matthew 24:3-14 is coming to fulfillment. The last portion of this passage speaks of the spreading of the Gospel, which we are beginning to see like no other time in history. This spirit of urgency and intercession that is over taking the Body of Christ is being closely followed by the spirit of evangelism, from stadiums to mega-tent meetings. Living with the belief that Jesus' return is sooner than we think, I am motivated to run this race with endurance and diligence. There is no time to waste; Jesus is indeed coming."

—Crystal Clarke
Full-time Intercessory Missionary
Orlando House of Prayer

Chapter 10

What Will It Be Like When Jesus Returns?

H ave you ever wondered what the days will look like just prior to the coming of the Lord? What will happen in the end times? The Bible is an amazing book, covering every aspect of life. It gives us profound wisdom, insight, and knowledge, instructing us how to live a successful life, both in God and in this world. Doctrine of the end times, embedded in Scripture, is of little value to most in the Body of Christ, who have very little, if any, knowledge of the last days' setting. According to Scripture, the days of the Son of Man will be filled with distinctions also characterized by the days of Noah and the days of Lot. In other words, if we simply study the days of Noah and Lot, we will glean insight into the days of the generation when Jesus returns. We will look at each of these days, described in the book of Luke, which have similar characteristics to the days just prior to the second coming of Christ.

> "For as the lightning that flashes out of one part under Heaven shines to the other part under Heaven, so also the Son of Man will be in His day . . . And as it was in the days of Noah, so it will be also in the days of the Son of Man . . . Likewise as it was also in the days of Lot: They ate, they drank, they bought, they sold, they planted, they built. . . Even so will it be in the day when the Son of Man is revealed."
>
> —*Luke 17:24, 26, 28, 30*

THE DAYS OF NOAH

The days of Noah are described in Genesis 6:11-13, depicting severe debauchery during the times in which he lived. We are told his generation was depraved before God and the earth was filled with violence. Before the Lord's eyes the earth was defiled, and all of humanity had corrupted its ways. As humans multiplied, increasing in numbers across the face of the earth, hearts were filled with all forms of perversion. Subsequently, God's Spirit declared He would not always strive with man; man's passions had begun to wildly depart from the path of righteousness. The Bible is not exactly clear as to the cause of this great wickedness, filling hearts with excessively evil self-centeredness, but the consequence for this degenerate state of mankind was the destruction of the earth by a flood. Only Noah, his family and two of every other kind of creature were saved in order to re-populate the earth.

There appears to have been some form of perverted mixture of the seed of man with what the Bible calls the *"sons of God"* and the *"daughters of men."* This mixture produced horrific consequences which spread throughout the whole earth. Some theologians believe there might have actually been an intermingling of demonic spirits with women, thereby creating a super-human race, demonically inspired, which threatened to destroy all of humanity, including the godly seed ordained to bring forth the birth of the Messiah through the family line of Seth.

> "There were giants on the earth in those days, and also afterward, when the sons of God came in to the daughters of men and they bore children to them. Those were the mighty men who were of old, men of renown. Then the Lord saw that the wickedness of man was great in the earth, and that every intent of the thoughts of his heart was only evil continually."
> —*Genesis 6:4-5*

So vast was the darkness covering the earth, the Bible tells us. Man's thoughts and passions were continually evil. This brought such great sorrow to the heart of God; He regretted His creation of man in the earth. When I observe modern society, I see the nations of the earth very close to the depths of iniquity and darkness that existed in the days of Noah. There is a day coming when the Lord will bring an end to life as we know it and He will establish His Kingdom in Jerusalem (Revelation 21:2-4, 10-27).

In Noah's day, God's patience had reached its limit, causing Him to declare the end of all flesh. The aforementioned scenario offers insight into the looming wickedness of a generation prior to Jesus' return. Motivated by redemption and love, the Lord will break forth in massive judgments against the nations of the earth. The book of Revelation gives the account of twenty-one different judgments that God will use to bring about the end of mankind as we know it, establishing the Kingdom of Christ, flooding the globe with righteousness to rule and reign (Revelation 6 through 18). God will use the Church as a major instrument to minister intercession, as she walks in her identity as a lover of God. The Church will be the messenger the Lord uses to reach the unsaved, prior to the second coming of Christ.

In the days of the Son of Man, God's intercession, through the Church, will release the burden of His heart, allowing her to work intimately with Him, to fellowship with Him and to partner with Him in the midst of a dark, violent hour. When there seems to be no hope for the people of the earth, she will be found standing in the gap.
(Revelation 5:8, 6:9-11, Joel 2:-14-19, Zephaniah 2:3)

In our culture we see many similarities with the evil characteristics that were prevalent in the days of Noah: violence of murder, abortion, robbery, sexual crime, war, etc. The list could go on and on. Abortion alone is one of the most horrific crimes against mankind today. Almost 60 million abortions take place worldwide each and every year, and one quarter of all pregnancies worldwide end in abortion. America has over 1.5 million babies aborted each year, with more than 4,100 taking place every single day. According to the Word of God, the shedding of blood is a form of violence, and from the ground it cries out to the Lord, demanding justice.

Another detestable form of violence manifesting itself is the breaking down of the family unit. The book of Malachi reveals that one of the most heinous crimes committed against the Godhead is divorce. Why? Divorce divides the family, seeking to destroy godly seed, hindering God's Spirit from raising up a generation to fill the earth. When a man and a woman become one in God's eyes through holy matrimony, God declares that no one should attempt to separate them. When divorce occurs, it is like ripping apart two people who are joined together in the flesh. Jesus said in Matthew 19:6 that no one should, *"Put asunder what God has joined together."* He was teaching about the horrors of divorce to those affected by it. The word, "asunder" actually means: *"To place room between; to part; to go away and to separate."* It is a violent act before the Lord, destroying families; therefore, God abhors it.

This is God's view of the destruction of the family unit which is being annihilated daily throughout our nation, in the form of divorce, resulting in the abandonment of our sons and daughters. God hates it! I know there are circumstances that may necessitate divorce, but according to Scripture, those are limited to unfaithfulness or abandonment in the marriage. Thank God for His mercy and His willingness to forgive the sins of both abortion and divorce. Today, however, it's simply too convenient to get a divorce for just about any reason. You don't like the way your spouse looks after 10 or 15 years into the marriage? No problem, there are thousands of divorce lawyers, who are ready to get you on the road to your new sense of freedom. It's so common to hear one spouse say, *"I don't love my wife anymore,"* or *"I'm tired of him,"* or *"We just don't get along."*

We must, therefore, remember the incredible miracle God did on our wedding day, when He took two individuals and made them one in spirit, one in soul, and one in body. When we seek a divorce, you can hear God saying, *"Don't destroy it. Don't rip it apart."* Why? It is because divorce is violent and it is the shedding of blood in His eyes. With over 50 percent of all Christian marriages ending in divorce, it's no wonder Jesus said that in the last days a, "brother shall betray his brother" (Mark 13:12). There will be no sense of loyalty, but instead, everyone will be looking out for their own benefit, at the expense of others (2 Timothy 3:1-5). Why? Because we have devalued what God has highly esteemed. How can the Church experience revival when we ignore so critical an issue as this?

Oh, how hypocritical we have been in the Church! On the one hand, we condemn the homosexual community for their lifestyle of immorality, but on the other hand, we flippantly get a divorce and move on to the next relationship, and then the next one, and then another one. We justify our own immorality at the expense of condemning others. Again, I know there are difficult conditions that might justify a divorce, but I am convinced that we are too quick to run to the courtroom to destroy what God intended to be a blessing to our lives and the lives of those around us. God cannot be any clearer when he says, *"I hate divorce."*

> "Yet you say, 'For what reason?' 'Because the Lord has been witness between you and the wife of your youth, with whom you have dealt treacherously; yet she is your companion and your wife by covenant. But did He not make them one, having a remnant of the Spirit? And why one? He seeks godly offspring. Therefore take heed to your spirit, and let none deal treacherously with the wife of his youth. For the Lord God of Israel says that He hates divorce, for it covers one's garment with violence,' Says the Lord of hosts. 'Therefore take heed to your spirit that you do not deal treacherously.'"
>
> —*Malachi 2:14-16*

THE DAYS OF LOT

In addition to the moral decay of society in Noah's day, the Bible describes conditions of the days of Abraham's nephew, Lot, as comparable to those prevailing in the generation of the Lord's return. From Scripture, we learn of the days of Lot as those during which people were self-absorbed, burning with the pleasures of life. They lived extravagant, sensual lifestyles, indulging in sexual appetites, detesting any consideration of putting away evil. They were consumed with buying and selling, trading and multiplying, while having little to no regard for the poor and needy, all around them. They were a loveless people, defrauding and oppressing the underprivileged. They accumulated more and more, while the poor among them became poorer and poorer.

Craving perversion was rampant, filling the earth with all kinds of deviant, sexual immoralities. The land itself became polluted, literally cursed. God had no choice but to purge the wickedness of Sodom and Gomorrah.

"Now before they lay down, the men of the city, the men of Sodom, both old and young, all the people from every quarter, surrounded the house. And they called to Lot and said to him, 'Where are the men who came to you tonight? Bring them out to us that we may know them carnally.'"

—*Genesis 19:4-5*

"Look, this was the iniquity of your sister Sodom: She and her daughter had pride, fullness of food, and abundance of idleness; neither did she strengthen the hand of the poor and needy."

—*Ezekiel 16:49*

"As Sodom and Gomorrah, and the cities around them in a similar manner to these, having given themselves over to sexual immorality and gone after strange flesh, are set forth as an example, suffering the vengeance of eternal fire."

—*Jude 1:7*

This was a direct assault on God's will and plans to raise a godly seed to be a witness in all the earth. Satan sought to disqualify those whom God had set apart by trying to tempt them into perversion, to draw them away through sensual desires, which would destroy their witness as the people of God. Revelation 9:21 sheds light on the major sins affecting the people of the earth prior to the coming of the Lord.

"And they did not repent of their murders or their sorceries or their sexual immorality or their thefts."

—*Revelation 9:21*

Further examination into chapter 9 of the book of Revelation reveals that verse 21 takes place after God has released a series of judgments, including six horrific trumpet blasts, each having severe tormenting plagues, causing major havoc to the empire of the antichrist and the nations of the earth. Despite the wrath of God being poured out, there will still be people who refuse to repent of their ways, and will choose instead to continue walking in their ways of darkness. They will be consumed with lust for immorality.

119

If you think the internet is bad right now, just give it another 10, 15, or 20 more years; the enemy will try to expose us to things so unimaginably evil. The enemy will seek to seduce and trap an entire generation to be continually exposed to destructive perversions. Can you envision what men will conjure and create once their consciences have been seared and their imaginations have run wild? It will be to the unthinkable depths of depravity. Laws will be passed that will protect and condone such atrocities, and the only sense of restraint will be what man determines is good or not good for himself. The days of immorality are increasing more and more, just as it did in the days of Lot.

Consider the evils of human trafficking. Over 80% of the human traffic victims are being forced into the rapidly growing sex industry, generating over $50 billion per year. There are estimates of about 35 million slaves on the earth today, and that number continues to climb at the alarming rate of 5 million per year. Some statistics claim that there could be as many as 100 to 200 million slaves on the earth today! How can it be in such a civilized world, that people would condone the slavery of little children and women, forcing them into sexual relations multiple times, on a daily basis? How can we expect God to turn away and not answer the cry of those being held captive against their will? How is it possible that we, the Church, called to be God's light and witness, sit idly by, not addressing the immorality we see all around us?

Pornography is nearly a $100 billion industry worldwide. There are nearly 5 million pornographic websites on the internet, with over 500 million pages containing pornographic material, viewable every second of every minute of every day. Every second, 30,000 internet users view pornographic pages, polluting their minds with perverse images of humanity. Homosexuality is sweeping across the globe, causing the nations of the earth to accept this lifestyle as an alternative to God's decree of union between a man and a woman. The Church is under great pressure to accept homosexuality as normal, and many denominations are even accepting homosexuals into the clergy and allowing them to be married in the Church.

The Apostle Paul prophesied that marriage would be outlawed in some places in the end times (1 Timothy 4:3). As horrific as current statistics appear, there is a swelling crescendo of great hope within the awakened Church. The sounds and songs of God are reverberating all around us. God has an answer, a solution to the darkness gripping the people of the world. He is stirring His awakened Church. She is once again returning to her first Love, to walk in the great commandment of loving God with all of her heart, soul, mind, and strength, and loving her neighbor as herself. She is rising to partner with God, walking in great revelation and understanding of the end times (Malachai 4:2-6 Acts 2:17-21, Revelation 22:17). The days of Noah and the days of Lot are now upon us, and their influence will continue to increase exponentially. However, there is also another day that is arising, and the Bible describes that day as the *"Day of the Son of Man."* This day releases the hope of eternal restoration to the nations of the earth. We will look into the "Days of the Son of Man" in the next chapter.

Before We Move On, Here Is Hope for the Hopeless, Help for the Helpless

Through the blood of Christ, *there is hope*, no matter your current or past circumstances. As painful and destructive as abortion, divorce, or any kind of perversion is to our lives, as well as in the eyes of the Lord, God specializes in making all things new. He will forgive and restore the lives of those who have been affected by sin. When we confess our sins and turn from them, God's word is clear: *He is faithful and just to forgive us of ALL our sins and to cleanse us from ALL unrighteousness.*

I have known individuals and families who have been devastated by sin, and I have seen first-hand as their lives were restored emotionally, physically, and mentally. I have witnessed the power of God raising them up and using them as vessels carrying His authority, as He speaks through them to bring healing to others affected by the same. The blood of Jesus is more powerful than any offense we can ever commit against God. We must, therefore, have faith and confidence in what He promises to do in us and through us because of what the blood of Jesus has already accomplished for us (Psalm 103:2-5, 12-14, Philippians 1:6, 1 John 1:9).

> Pray this, if you will: "Father, I believe Your Word, and I rec-
> ognize my sin has separated me from You. I repent of the sin
> of _____, and ask for the blood of Christ to cleanse me from

all my sin, cleanse me from all guilt and shame, and make me whole. From this day forward, I choose to follow hard after You! I choose to commit my heart and my life to You! Lead me in the paths of righteousness, for Your Name's sake. In the Name of Jesus, I pray, I believe, and I receive, Amen.

"When I first came on staff at the Orlando House of Prayer, I remember setting aside Mondays exclusively for studying the book of Revelation. As I was prayerfully studying this book, one thing became clear to me: this book is truly the Revelation of Jesus Christ. Before then, my approach to this book was mainly to debate my point or just to expand my biblical knowledge. Not once had I seen it as the Revelation of His wisdom, leadership, glory and power that would be fully revealed in the day of His return. My mindset was similar to that of the Pharisees when Jesus told them, 'You have your heads in your Bibles constantly because you think you'll find eternal life there. But you miss the forest for the trees. These Scriptures are all about Me! And here I am, standing right before you, and you aren't willing to receive from Me the life you say you want' (John 5:39-40, The Message).

Could it be true that with us being so concerned with charts, predictions, and judgments that we have lost sight of Christ? When we lose sight of Him, we lose sight of the very hope of our calling, the hope of our salvation and the hope of our glory. It's my heart to see a witness go forth that will turn a generation back to 'Behold the Lamb' in all of His glory and beauty."

—Mark Helligar
Full-time Intercessory Missionary
Orlando House of Prayer

Chapter 11

How Jesus' Day Is the Hope
of the Nations

W e have seen from Luke's writings what it will be like in the day Jesus returns to the earth. As it was in the days of Noah and in the days of Lot, the negative characteristics of those days will be greatly multiplied in the day of the Son of Man when Jesus returns. Despite all the darkness and wickedness filling the nations in that generation, God has declared this vow: In the midst of the greatest darkness in the earth, there will be hope and salvation for the world. Just when it looks like the enemy will have his way and completely wipe out any hope of God's eternal plan being fulfilled; the God of the universe will break in with His might and power, bringing complete restoration of the eternal plan of God for the earth.

The second coming of Christ is the only hope the world can have in a time and hour of vile wickedness, as iniquity floods and overwhelms the people of the earth. In His wisdom, God has planned for the Church of Jesus Christ to become His partner, the vessel He will use to help bring about God's will into the earth. Let's look at three key characteristics of the *"Day of the Son of Man,"* that will help the Church play an integral role, bringing forth the will of Heaven to the Earth and ushering in the coming of Christ.

1. THE CHURCH'S AWAKENING DESIRE FOR JESUS

One of the most profound prophetic promises of God we are beginning to see come to pass in our day is the burning desire in the heart of the Church to encounter the love of God in an experiential manner. In other words, the Church is beginning to wake up and realize, unless the love of God burns and consumes her, she will neither be equipped nor ready to face the darkest hour the earth is about to encounter. While teaching on the end times, Jesus said that the Church would come to the place where she would begin to *desire* to see one of the days of the Son of Man (Luke 17:22). In the Greek the word, "desire" means, *"to set the heart upon; to long for; to covet; to lust after."* It is a strong word that describes burning, consuming, fiery passion overtaking an individual, causing them to vigorously pursue the very object of affection, no matter the cost.

This is the heart posture the Church will come to in the day prior to the coming of the Lord. The Apostle Paul said he longed to be with the Lord, rather than to continue living here on the earth (Philippians 1:23). Paul had this revelation and understood what it meant to be completely overcome and given over to being a person in pursuit of the presence of Christ.

"The Days of the Son of Man" refer to the prophetic hour when the Church will be awakened to love and be stirred to walk in the intimacy in which she was destined to walk. God intended for man to walk in intimacy with Him from the beginning of creation. He has continually sought man, so man could walk in the fullness of his destiny and manifest the will of God on the earth. We see Jesus rebuking the Church of Ephesus for not continuing in the love of Christ. Although the Church of Ephesus was known to do great works for the Lord as a prominent revival center of the earth in that day, she eventually began to put more emphasis on doing the works of God than loving the God who empowered them to do His works in the first place. He strongly corrected them, warning them that unless they repented and returned back to the place of loving God first, He would have to remove their lampstand from its place. In other words, the strength and ability to successfully do God's work is rooted and grounded in the reality of having a burning passion for the Person of Christ. Our witness is only as effective as the fire of God burning in the lampstand of our hearts.

> "I know your works, your labor, your patience, and that you cannot bear those who are evil. And you have tested those who say they are apostles and are not, and have found them liars . . . Nevertheless, I have this against you, that you have left your first love. Remember therefore from where you have

fallen; repent and do the first works, or else I will come to you quickly and remove your lampstand from its place—unless you repent."

—*Revelation 2:2, 4-5*

THE FIRST WEDDING AT CREATION

The Bible reveals a God who is so passionate about walking in intimacy with His creation that He beautifully communicates it through the picture of a wedding (Genesis 1:28, 2:18-25). The book of Genesis tells us God's highest creation was not the moon, the sun, the stars, the animals or the fish of the sea; His greatest creation was mankind. Of all of God's creations, man is the only created being into which God breathed His life and fashioned into His own image and likeness (Genesis 1:26-27).

Once God had made Adam, He immediately began to look for the perfect helpmate, who could walk alongside Adam and help him fulfill the longing of his heart and the purpose of creation. Adam was not complete until he became one with Eve (Genesis 2:23-24). This clearly purposes the passion of God's heart to partner with man in flooding the earth with the knowledge of God and the righteousness of His Kingdom. The Apostle Paul also wrote about the relationship between a man and a woman and its symbolism relating to the ultimate relationship between God and man (Ephesians 5:22-33).

"Husbands, love your wives, just as Christ also loved the Church and gave Himself for her . . . For this reason a man shall leave his father and mother and be joined to his wife, and the two shall become one flesh. This is a great mystery, but I speak concerning Christ and the Church."

—*Ephesians 5:25, 31-32*

THE FIRST MIRACLE AT A WEDDING

We see that the first reference of man in the book of Genesis is in the context of a wedding. It's not surprising that Jesus' first recorded miracle in all of the New Testament just happens to be at the wedding of Cana in Galilee. Think of it: Of all the miracles Jesus could have performed as His first, God chose for the initial miracle to be demonstrated at a wedding. By instructing the servants to fill six stone pots with water, primarily used for purification of guests, Jesus turns the filled pots of water into wine. Jesus' miracle of turning water into wine took place when the master of the feast did not have enough wine for all his guests. When the master and guests of the feast were presented with new wine, they were amazed the best wine was reserved for last, rather than served at the beginning.

The Holy Spirit indicates prophetically that the greatest wine, which will bring everlasting joy, is reserved for the end times.

This best wine reserved for last also speaks of God's intention to release the greatest revelations for the Church, as she walks in her identity as the Bride of Christ, resulting in true cleansing of the heart of man.

The First Wedding In the Millennial Kingdom

The Lord is wooing the Bride of Christ to desire Him once again in preparation for the greatest wedding at the end of the age. The Holy Spirit is preparing the Church, requiring the great commandment, so the Church may walk in the fullness of the love of God and keep the commandments of God. Jesus said in John 14:15, if we loved Him, we would keep His Word. The secret to living out God's Word is a life of obedience, walking out the great commandment, and loving God first, with all our heart, soul, mind, and strength (Mark 12:30). God's Spirit has been given to us as a Helper on this side of eternity, in order for us to walk side-by-side with the Lord. As the Helper, the Holy Spirit deposits the love of God in us, so we cannot help but love Him in return. We display this love for Him by desiring to live a lifestyle of obedience to His Word.

> "If you love Me, keep My commandments. And I will pray the Father, and He will give you another Helper, that He may abide with you forever."
>
> —*John 14:15-16*

When it is all said and done, the burden of the Lord will be fulfilled, as the Church of Jesus will have learned to walk in complete unity with one another and in submission to the will of God for herself and for the earth. The work of the Holy Spirit is clearly evident throughout the book of Revelation, as He prepares the Church to become the Bride of Christ. The great work of the Spirit in the Church is to empower her not only to exhibit God's gifts and power, but also to display the fruit of the Spirit. He will take the Church through spiritual disciplines until she manifests the character of the Son of God as mature believers.

> *By awakening the Church to her first love,*
> *the Holy Spirit will make her ready, prepared and fit*
> *for the greatest hour the Church will ever face...*

The Church will abandon herself in complete surrender to the love of God, so that she may be greatly used to release God's power in the last days (Revelation 19:6-9). The cry of the Church will be to grow to fullness, until the burning desire in her heart is in complete agreement and unison with the cry of the Spirit, who expresses the depth of the heart of the eternal Godhead.

> "And the Spirit and the Bride say, 'Come!' And let him who hears say, 'Come!' And let him who thirsts come. Whoever desires, let him take the water of life freely."
>
> —*Revelation 22:17*

2. The Church's Expectation of the Coming of the Lord

Jesus cautions us not to believe every doctrine about His coming, or we might be in danger of being easily swayed away from walking intimately with God. Heeding false eschatology will cause us to lose sight of the signs of the times that point to the second coming of Christ. Luke tells us Jesus' return will be as the lightning flashes out of one part under Heaven and shines to the other part under Heaven. It will be a sudden appearing, and only those prepared will be ready, in expectation of His return.

The *"Days of the Son of Man"* will be filled with great deception, causing mankind to either dismiss the urgency of the hour completely, or scoff at the idea that the Son of God will return to establish His Kingdom on the earth. Those in the Church that are living such carefree lives will be clueless to the doctrine of the second coming of Christ. The majority of the Church today has no interest in eschatology or the importance of its doctrine; therefore, the Church will find herself in an unprepared state. She will not be found standing strong as the voice of God in a deceived and confused generation, for she, herself, has been deceived and lulled to sleep.

In his famous Olivet Discourse, Jesus sat with his disciples on the Mount of Olives, teaching them the signs of the times at the end of the age. The first key sign that Jesus gave in His teaching was to warn His disciples about the great deception in the days just prior to His return. This deception would be rooted in a lack of knowing and loving Christ intimately.

The lack of loving Christ and the lack of making Him priority opens our hearts and minds to the spirit of deception. Therefore, Jesus warns us to beware of false christ's, who would come to deceive many, creating their own following. How could this happen to followers of Christ who claim to be His disciples? How could the enemy deceive God's people in the first place? He does so by luring us away through distractions of the heart, which cause our souls to long for and seek after things other than Him.

This leads to a message that promotes false intimacy, which tells us we can be right with God without submitting ourselves to His leadership, and without having our hearts ravished by His love for us.

Thus, an atmosphere is cultivated in which the pleasures of life rise and take prominent place in the hearts of humanity; as a result, lawlessness will increase and the love of many will grow cold.

Unfortunately, this will even affect the Body of Christ, which will lead to the great falling away, setting up the perfect scenario for the antichrist to establish his kingdom (2 Thessalonians 2:3). His leadership and policies will appeal to the heart of the nations, deceiving many even in the Church, who will be sucked into his lies and his philosophy of pleasure (2 Timothy 3:1-5). This will deceive countless hearts in the Church, eventually leading to a great division between the lukewarm believer and the one whose heart has been conquered by the love of Christ.

> "Then many false prophets will rise up and deceive many. And because lawlessness will abound, the love of many will grow cold."
>
> —*Matthew 24:11-12*

The Apostle Paul greatly emphasized the urgent need for the Church to be well grounded and established in doctrines of the last days. He prophesied that the earth would be filled with great deception as satan would promote doctrines of demons, causing many to heed deceiving spirits, searing the conscience of man, causing him to pursue the pleasures of life, and rejecting God's right to the heart of mankind (1 Timothy 4:1-2).

The Church at Thessalonica was well grounded in the teaching of eschatology. Paul reminded them that Jesus would come as a thief in the night, and many would be caught off guard, not ready for His return. He reminded them of the importance of living righteous, pure lives because they were children of the light and not children of the darkness. He knew that living unholy lives would dull the spirit of man, keeping him from the ability to discern correctly the signs of the times. (1 Thessalonians 4:13-5:11, 2 Thessalonians 2:1-12).

There is power in living pure and holy lives before the Lord, as it positions the spirit of man to have clear communication lines with the Spirit of God. As our lives are sanctified and holy unto the Lord, we protect ourselves from the spirit of this age and the spirit of deception. There are great promises in Scripture to those who choose to live holy lives. These promises release revelations of God and help us to see and know His will and to discern the generation in which we live.

> "Blessed are the pure in heart, for they shall see God."
>
> —*Matthew 5:8*

"Pursue peace with all people, and holiness, without which no one will see the Lord."

—Hebrews 12:14

"Beloved, now we are children of God; and it has not yet been revealed what we shall be, but we know that when He is revealed, we shall be like Him, for we shall see Him as He is. And everyone who has this hope in Him purifies himself, just as He is pure."

—1 John 3:2-3

Living our lives sanctified for the purposes of God positions us to have our spiritual ears open to fresh revelations from the Holy Spirit. This includes revelations about the end times, which according to prophetic writings, will increase in the last days (Daniel 12:4, 10). It is our right and inheritance to know what's in the heart of God and what His will is for the earth. Therefore, it will be a necessity for the End-Time Church to walk in understanding concerning the signs of our Lord's return (Matthew 16:1-3, Luke 21:25).

Why would Jesus teach His disciples to watch out for the signs if He was not intending them to be prepared and ready for His return? Why would the Apostle Paul emphasize teaching on the second coming if he was not convinced that the Church could be found in a state of readiness? The book of Daniel reveals that the people of God in the last days would grow in great knowledge and understanding concerning things that have been sealed and unknown for generations. Daniel longed to fully understand what would take place in the days prior to the coming of the Lord. The angel Gabriel revealed to him that such revelations were set aside for the people living in that day and God would make sure His people would increase in knowledge and understanding of end time eschatology. This is a direct reference to the ministry of the Holy Spirit, whose job description is to prepare the Church and equip her by revealing to her things yet to come.

"But you, Daniel, shut up the words, and seal the book until the time of the end; many shall run to and fro, and knowledge

131

shall increase . . . And he said, 'Go your way, Daniel, for the words are closed up and sealed till the time of the end.'"

—*Daniel 12:4,9*

"However, when He, the Spirit of truth, has come, He will guide you into all truth; for He will not speak on His own *authority,* but whatever He hears He will speak; and He will tell you things to come."

—*John 16:13*

3. The Church's Partnership With God to Bring Justice to the Earth

In the previous chapter, I shared the descriptions found in the book of Luke that reveal similar conditions in the day of the Lord's return. He writes what Jesus taught concerning the days of Noah and the days of Lot, which were marked by rampant, lascivious living. Luke compares the days of Noah and Lot to the days immediately before Christ returns. In the same manner that the people would not heed the warnings of Abraham and Noah, many today will choose to dismiss the warnings that will come through the Church.

Nonetheless, God will do everything He can to avert the inevitable judgment that will be released upon the end time generation. Their continual pursuit of pleasure and wickedness will ripen them to receive the wrath and judgments of God. Jesus compared the sudden judgments released upon the two generations of Lot and Noah saying, *"It will be so in the day when the Son of Man is revealed"* (Luke 17:26-30). This has specific reference to the twenty-one judgments taught in the book of Revelation, as part of God's cleansing and purging procedure to rid the earth of all wickedness and rebellion of mankind against God and His Kingdom.

A study of the seven seals, seven trumpets, and seven bowls of God's judgments reveal the Church responding to God's invitation, partnering with Him as He releases judgments and brings forth His justice throughout the four corners of the earth. The Church's prayers and cries for justice will bring relief and righteousness to the Church. To the wicked, justice comes in the form of judgment (Luke 18:1-7). Answered prayers are justice to the righteous and judgment to the wicked.

Much like God used the intercession of Moses and Aaron to release the ten plagues in Egypt, bringing deliverance and salvation to the Jewish nation, so also it will be in the day Jesus is revealed. God will once again turn to His people, the Church, the redeemed and they will partner with Him in the ministry of intercession, thus releasing the twenty-one judgments that will completely rid the earth of all evil and darkness. This will give way to the Kingdom of God being established in the millennial reign of Christ.

> "Then another angel, having a golden censer, came and stood at the altar. He was given much incense that he should offer it with the prayers of all the saints upon the golden altar, which was before the throne. And the smoke of the incense, with the prayers of the saints, ascended before God from the angel's hand. Then the angel took the censer, filled it with fire from the altar, and threw it to the earth. And there were noises, thunderings, lightnings, and an earthquake."
>
> —*Revelation 8:3-5*

> "Now I saw Heaven opened, and behold, a white horse. And He who sat on him was called Faithful and True, and in righteousness He judges and makes war. His eyes were like a flame of fire, and on His head were many crowns. He had a name written that no one knew except Himself. He was clothed with a robe dipped in blood, and His name is called The Word of God. And the armies in Heaven, clothed in fine linen, white and clean, followed Him on white horses. Now out of His mouth goes a sharp sword, that with it He should strike the nations. And He Himself will rule them with a rod of iron. He Himself treads the winepress of the fierceness and wrath of Almighty God. And He has on His robe and on His thigh a name written: King of Kings and Lord of Lords."
>
> —*Revelation 19:11-16*

The work of the Holy Spirit in the end times will reveal God's heart and love to the Church, quickening her to pursue Him in extravagant devotion and total abandonment, causing His justice to fill all of the earth. Jesus reveals Himself as a God who is a Bridegroom, pursuing the Church in love and transforming her into a mature Bride, equipped and prepared for the darkest hour in all of history. This revelation will eventually lead to His revelation in the sky, when the sixth seal is opened and the inhabitants of the earth see His wrath being unleashed. Citizens of the earth will unsuccessfully seek to hide themselves from the wrath of the Lamb and from the great day of God's judgments.

> "I looked when He opened the sixth seal, and behold, there was a great earthquake; and the sun became black as sackcloth of hair, and the moon became like blood. And the stars of Heaven fell to the earth, as a fig tree drops its late figs when it is shaken by a mighty wind. Then the sky receded as a scroll when it is rolled up, and every mountain and island was moved out of its place. And the kings of the earth, the great men, the rich men, the commanders, the mighty men, every slave and every free man, hid themselves in the caves and in the rocks of the mountains, and said to the mountains and rocks, 'Fall on us and hide us from the face of Him who sits on the throne and from the wrath of the Lamb! For the great day of His wrath has come, and who is able to stand?'"
>
> —*Revelation 6:12-17*

Let us, therefore, seek the Lord with all of our hearts that our lives may be found watching and waiting for His return. Let us turn from any questionable activity that works to guide our hearts away from His cause and purpose for our lives.

Maranatha!
Even so, come Lord Jesus, come!

"My wife received a dream from the Lord about great intimidation and false wonders coming from the evil one towards God's people. In her dream, she was in a group of very strong-spirited, influential men and women of God. All of a sudden, false signs appeared in the heavens and great fear overcame the saints of God. My wife, operating in her authority in Christ, boldly rebuked the false spirit. Immediately, it stopped.

This dream speaks volumes to the Bride of Christ: She should know who she is and Who is living inside of her. As the Bride of Christ, we must not allow the intimidation of the enemy to steal away our identity in Christ.

As intercessors and worship leaders at the House of Prayer in Orlando, it is the cry of our hearts to see the Lord receive the reward of His suffering and to see His great desire fulfilled at His coming. As friends of God, our hearts are gripped with the reality that the state of the Church and of society are not okay, and they won't be, in full measure, until He returns. Like John the Baptist, the greatest man born of a woman outside of Jesus, we have committed our lives to prepare the way for His second coming. Through a lifestyle of consistent holiness, fasting, intercession, and humility, my wife and I have laid down our lives to see Him restore all things at His coming; to see the glorious day of His appearing."

—Jaime & Jessica Tosado
Full-time Intercessory Missionaries
Orlando House of Prayer

Section Five:
The Spirit-Filled Life—"The Next Great Move of My Spirit."

I wondered, "How is it possible that I would not be ready for a great move of God's Spirit and power?"

I thrived on being a man of the Spirit and seeing the manifestation of His anointing throughout my ministry. The faithful Holy Spirit revealed to me that what was coming would require great humility, character and a hatred for self-glorification. The humility and power of the risen Christ will be greatly expressed by servants desiring to glorify Christ.

Chapter Twelve

Getting Reacquainted With the Holy Spirit

In my encounter with the Lord in 2005, one of the things that shocked me the most was when the Lord said to me that I would not be personally ready to participate in the next great outpouring and move of the Holy Spirit that He was planning to release all across the earth. I believe many, if not most, in the Body of Christ have neglected the Person, work and ministry of the Holy Spirit in their journey of faith and throughout their Christian life. The ministry of the Holy Spirit is one of the most misunderstood ministries in the Church today. As a result, many believers are disqualifying themselves from the work of God's power that He is stirring in the earth today.

After it is all said and done, one must conclude that without the influence of God's Spirit, darkness would completely cover the earth and misery would fill all the nations. It is for this purpose that God has anointed His Church in order that the powers of evil could be vanquished and the testimony of Jesus could be seen and heard throughout the world. The initial work of the Holy Spirit in the unconverted is to bring the sinner to the point of recognizing his need for Christ. The Spirit then seeks to sanctify and empower the convert, that he may become a vessel of honor and be useful for God's purposes. Understanding the role of the Holy Spirit throughout the different phases of our spiritual walk will help us greatly in knowing how God's Spirit will take us from one level of glory to another level of glory and power. There are three main phases that each believer goes through from the time the Spirit deals with them in their sinful state until the time that He fills them with His power and anointing.

1. THE HOLY SPIRIT IS *WITH US*

Before we were ever a part of God's family, the Spirit of God was actively working on our hearts to bring us to the point where we would see our need to accept Christ as our Savior. Prior to the work of salvation, the Holy Spirit is simply WITH US to open up our spiritual eyes to our own need of God's salvation plan of forgiveness for all of humanity. This is how each man and woman is dealt with by the Lord. Jesus said that He would send the Spirit after His resurrection for the purpose of dealing with the hearts of sinners in three specific ways.

The first main work of the Holy Spirit is to bring every unbeliever into the Body of Christ through His power and ability to convict the sinner of their sin. Once convicted, the unbeliever begins to look for a way of escape and a solution to his problem of sin. This is when the Holy Spirit begins to reveal the sacrifice of Jesus on the Cross on behalf of the convicted sinner (Ephesians 2:1-3).

Secondly, once convinced of their need for forgiveness, the Spirit begins to reveal the righteousness of Christ and our lack of it. He begins to reveal to us our own depravity in light of Christ's perfect holiness (Romans 3:23).

Finally, once we are convinced of our own sin and lack of righteousness to meet God's holy standards, the Spirit reveals to us the judgment that awaits us unless we repent and turn from our sins. For the first time the sinner begins to see that his sin has eternally separated him from God and therefore realizes that death and eternal judgment is the only recompense for his own depravity (Romans 23).

> "Nevertheless I tell you the truth. It is to your advantage that I go away; for if I do not go away, the Helper will not come to you; but if I depart, I will send Him to you. And when He has come, He will convict the world of sin, and of righteousness, and of judgment: of sin, because they do not believe in Me; of righteousness, because I go to My Father and you see Me no more; of judgment, because the ruler of this world is judged."
>
> *—John 16:7-11*

Most people in the Body of Christ have taken for granted the work of the Holy Spirit in their lives. As a result, He is neglected and not given the rightful place in the life of every believer; a place in which He desires to lead and guide their lives in sweet, Holy Communion with the Lord. The Holy Spirit is treated more as a spiritual force rather than a person. From the moment that we first accepted Christ as our Savior until the moment that Jesus returns to receive us unto Himself, the Holy Spirit is the One who seeks to bring us into spiritual maturity and to the place where all that God has for us can be fully accomplished in us. All this is possible because He is committed to finishing the entire work of our salvation in our lives. His miracle of the "new creation" (2 Corinthians 5:17) beautifully works regeneration within us (Titus 3:5), reconciling us to our Heavenly Father (Romans 5:10) and making us part of His family through the miraculous act of adoption as He receives us into His family as His very own (Romans 8:15). This is all possible because the Spirit is continually WITH US, seeking to bring the unbeliever into Christ.

2. THE HOLY SPIRIT IN US

The work of salvation continues in the life of the new believer as the Holy Spirit now takes residence in the heart of every newborn child of God. This phase of the Spirit's work comes from the Holy Spirit, not just being with us, but now coming to live IN US in the heart of every Christian. It is at this point that we become the temple of God. In essence, just as Christ tabernacled among His disciples, God is now tabernacling among us through the Person of the Holy Spirit's indwelling. This is why Jesus said that it would be better for Him to depart so that He could send the disciples another Comforter. Jesus was speaking about the Person of the Holy Spirit, Who would not only be with His followers but now would be living inside of them.

> "The Spirit of truth, whom the world cannot receive, because it neither sees Him nor knows Him; but you know Him, for He dwells with you and will be in you."
>
> —*John 14:17*

EXACTLY WHAT DOES THE WORK OF THE HOLY SPIRIT SEEK TO ACCOMPLISH IN US?

ONCE WE ARE SAVED FROM OUR SINS, THE SPIRIT BEGINS TO DEAL WITH THE SOUL OF THE BELIEVER FOR THE PURPOSE OF BRINGING THE WORK OF SANCTIFICATION INTO THE HEART OF THE CHRISTIAN.

He does this by speaking truth to our inner man that causes us to confront areas of weakness and carnality. There is a need to rid ourselves from our former life and old nature in order for us to encounter the deeper truths of God's ways. This is why it is vital for the believer to have a daily intake of God's word. It is through the word of God that the Holy Spirit speaks to the heart of the individual, seeking to point him in the way of truth. As the Holy Spirit speaks the truth of God's word to us we are given the choice of either obeying or rejecting the truth about our spiritual condition and whether or not we desire to go deeper in measures of consecration (Psalm 119:9-11; John 17:17-17).

OUR COOPERATION WITH THE SPIRIT'S WORK IN US CAUSES US TO BE CONFORMED TO THE IMAGE OF THE SON OF GOD.

This is the ultimate work of the Holy Spirit inside the heart of the believer. The Spirit seeks to make us more like Christ by causing our very lives to reflect the character of Jesus that allows us to shine brightly as testimonies of the Lord. We desperately need to allow the Spirit of God to finish the work of sanctification in our lives. Many believers seek after God's power and the nine *gifts* of the Holy Spirit, while all along rejecting His work of producing the nine *fruits* of the Holy Spirit, which are a reflection of the character of Christ in us (1 Corinthians 12:7-11; Galatians 5:22-25).

DEEPER LEVELS OF GOD'S PRESENCE AND GOD'S GLORY

After encountering God's presence over and over again, Moses' face began to shine and radiate from the presence of the glory of God. Much like this, the work of transformation becomes evident to others around us as we reflect the glory of God like Moses did. Other instances of this were recorded in Scripture as well; the apostles in the book of Acts were recognized by the religious leaders of their day to have been with Jesus because they saw their open boldness of faith and willingness to witness to all who would hear (Acts 4:13, 2 Corinthians 3:17-18).

THE HOLY SPIRIT'S DEEP WORKS OF SANCTIFICATION BY THE SPIRIT OF GOD SEALS US UNTO THE DAY OF JUDGMENT

There is a place the believer can come to where he walks in great confidence and does not fear the coming of the Lord and the judgments He will disburse at His coming. As a result of the work of sanctification in our inner man, the Spirit of God brings us great assurance of our acceptance in Christ until the end. The Greek word for sealed is, *"sfag-id-zo"* which is defined, *"to stamp (as with a signet or private mark) for security or preservation; to keep secret."* God claims us as His own and secures us from the coming judgment that the world and the unbeliever will be facing in the day of God's wrath (Ephesians 4:30).

THE ANOINTING/GOD'S POWER UPON US

Having made His home in us, the Holy Spirit strives to get us to yield to His leadership and allow the Spirit of Lordship to rule our lives. As He produces the character of Christ in us, He transforms us into the image of Christ so that He may fully entrust us with God's power UPON US. We see from the book of Acts the results and the power that was demonstrated by the early Church after the Holy Spirit filled the 120 believers in the upper room. Their massive success caused them to be accused of having turned the world upside down with their passionate fervor for sharing the Gospel of Christ. What is the secret to their success? The Holy Spirit coming upon them! Jesus had promised His disciples that they would be filled with the Person of the Holy Spirit and would receive His power to perform signs and wonders (Matthew 28:18-20, Mark 16:17-20, Luke 24:49, John 14:12, Acts 1:4-8, 2:1-4, 16-21). He taught them of the importance of being baptized with the promise of the Father, Who He also called, the Comforter (John 14:26).

> "Behold, I send the Promise of My Father upon you; but tarry in the city of Jerusalem until you are endued with power from on high."
>
> —*Luke 24:49*

To be *"endued"* with the power of the Spirit means to clothe oneself and be arrayed with the power of God as one would put on a piece of clothing. The fullness of the infilling of the Holy Spirit includes being filled from within and being engulfed with His power on the outside of us. In other words, the Holy Spirit will come upon the believer the same way a man puts on a garment. We are given the assurance that when the Holy Spirit comes upon us He will help us to have victory in every area of our lives. The Holy Spirit also helps us to walk in our new identity as He teaches us to *"put on the new man."* This *"new man"* is created according to God's power in true righteousness and holiness (Ephesians 4:24). It is through the Holy Spirit that we are also able to *"put on"* the armor of God. By doing so, He helps us to resist the powers of darkness. Through the anointing, we are able to break off all forms of satanic attacks and lies against us (Ephesians 6:11). The Holy Spirit also assists us to *"put on"* the Lord Jesus Christ. This strengthens us to overcome all temptations of the flesh. The Spirit lives inside of us so He is constantly reminding us of who we are in Christ and who Christ is in us. He is always pointing to Jesus as the great testifier of what He has done in our lives (Romans 13:14).

THE BAPTISM IN THE HOLY SPIRIT

Our relationship with the Holy Spirit is vitally important if we are to live overcoming lives in our Christian walk. To help illustrate this, imagine an empty cup. This empty cup symbolizes the life of a person who does not have the life of God living inside of them. They are empty of God's presence and are separated from God. The moment a person repents of their sin, the Spirit of God comes to live inside of them. Depending on how we respond to His work, we determine the measure of our fullness with the life of the Spirit.

> *Some believers have their cup partially filled with the life of God and therefore live somewhat defeated in their walk with God.*

Others have learned to yield to the Spirit's leadership and have their cup filled with the life of God and walk in a measure of great victory because they have allowed the spirit of discipline to lead and guide them. There is still yet a greater experience we can all encounter: When you fill up an empty wine glass with water, the water will float within the glass and fill it up. Now take that same wine glass, and submerge it in a whole pool of water; now, the wine glass is not just filled up on the inside, it is entirely baptized in the water, inside and out! This is an example of a believer who has the Spirit in him *and* upon him. The cup at the bottom of the pool is not just filled; it is completely baptized in the water! This is the life of the believer who has learned to overcome against sin's temptation and is also walking in a measure of power and anointing in the baptism of the Holy Spirit. Jesus clearly said to His disciples that they were to receive power after the Holy Spirit came upon them.

> "But you shall receive power when the Holy Spirit has come upon you; and you shall be witnesses to Me in Jerusalem, and in all Judea and Samaria, and to the end of the earth."
>
> —*Acts 1:8*

The word for *"power"* in Acts 1:8 means, *"to have force; miraculous power; ability; abundance; a worker of miracles; strength; violence."* It is the Greek word, *"dunamis,"* from which we get the English word for dynamite. The believer has to come to the place where they realize God's miraculous power resides inside of them. This power is for the purpose of making us into effective witnesses for Christ. It is for this reason that the Spirit of God is able to work miracles through the life of those who believe that God's power is still available for us today. Unfortunately, some believe that God's anointing and His power are no longer active today in the Church. In places where the anointing and the baptism of the Holy Spirit are an everyday experience, people are seeing miracles take place as they did in the book of Acts. If we are going to experience God's victory in this day and hour and in the years to come, we must once again reacquaint ourselves with the Person, work and ministry of the Holy Spirit. Powers of darkness are becoming bolder and bolder and God's people must rise up to fulfill the Great Commission with the power of the Holy Spirit.

"Being in an environment where Holy Spirit can move freely through the exaltation of Jesus Christ has radically changed my life. Joining staff at OHOP, I've grown in the realization of His existence and qualities. As I'm reacquainted with the person of the Holy Spirit, I live a more sacrificial life unto my Savior and Friend, Jesus Christ. In the context of night-and-day prayer, my heart is encountered daily with this truth. When Jesus is lauded, the Holy Spirit comes with revelation. I have spent countless hours basking myself in His presence and am convinced that the prayer room is one of the most important tools I can use to connect with Him in an intimate way. It serves as a spiritual greenhouse, where a continual aroma is being offered up, creating a sweet atmosphere for fellowship. I am extremely thankful for the ministry of worship and prayer that promotes unity of the Spirit."

—Eliezer Perez
Full-time Intercessory Missionary
Orlando House of Prayer

Chapter Thirteen

The Urgent Need For a Spirit-Filled People

There is an urgent need for Christians to become vessels of supernatural ministry by functioning in spiritual gifts and operating in the authority of Christ. Faith comes by hearing and hearing by the word of God (Romans 10:17). Therefore, it is vital for the Church to study and understand the gifts of the Spirit and His anointing. Jesus does not want the Church to be ignorant of the spiritual gifts; however, we will never function in God's power until we earnestly desire to be used by God. As we seek God's face, we experience intimacy with Him; as we seek His hand, we release His power through the gifts and anointing of the Holy Spirit upon our lives. It is, therefore, necessary for us to desire the spiritual gifts that are revealed to us in 1 Corinthians 12. We need to pray to receive His spiritual gifts in order for them to begin to operate freely in our lives. The Lord presents opportunities for us to release His power in everyday circumstances of life (1 Corinthians 12:31, 14:1, 39).

THE PROMISE OF AN END TIME OUTPOURING OF GOD'S SPIRIT

Both the Old and New Testaments prophetically point to a day when the Holy Spirit will be poured out in such a way that all the nations of the earth will submit to the leadership of Jesus in the millennial Kingdom (Psalm 72). The Old Testament prophets spoke of a time when the knowledge of the Lord and His power would cover the face of the earth (Isaiah 11:9, Habakkuk 2:4). We have seen a partial fulfillment of that, 2000 years ago, on the day of Pentecost, when the 120 disciples of the Lord were baptized in the Holy Spirit. This was an actual fulfillment of a prophetic word given by the Prophet Joel, and again confirmed by the Apostle Peter.

"And it shall come to pass afterward that I will pour out My Spirit on all flesh; your sons and your daughters shall prophesy, your old men shall dream dreams, your young men shall see visions. And also on My menservants and on My maidservants I will pour out My Spirit in those days."

—*Joel 2:28-29*

"But this is what was spoken by the prophet Joel: 'And it shall come to pass in the last days, says God, that I will pour out of My Spirit on all flesh; your sons and your daughters shall prophesy, your young men shall see visions, your old men shall dream dreams. And on My menservants and on My maidservants I will pour out My Spirit in those days; And they shall prophesy.'"

—*Acts 2:16-18*

Both Joel and Peter spoke of a time when God's Spirit would be poured out upon all flesh, and not just upon the Jewish believers. This shocked the Jewish disciples, as they realized the Holy Spirit was also being offered to Gentile believers (Acts 10). Herein, lays the beautiful aspect of the promise of the Spirit: There are no restrictions and anyone is eligible to partake in the promised blessing. In other words, the young and the old, male and female, Jew and Gentile all share the privilege of receiving the Holy Spirit's baptism when they put their faith and trust in Jesus Christ (Acts 2:38-39).

One, therefore, cannot question the great success of the early Church in flooding the Roman Empire with the message of the Gospel of Christ, with Holy Spirit's confirmation through His manifested power. The early apostles did not simply present nice little messages; their preaching and teaching were strongly endorsed by demonstration of the Spirit's power. Evidence of supernatural activity is clearly seen throughout the book of Acts. This powerful book could easily be called *"The Acts of the Holy Spirit"* (Acts 3:1-9, 4:23-37, 5:1-12, 17-42, 6:2-7, 8-10, 54-60, 8:4-25, 26-40, 9:1-18, 31, 32-35, 36-42, 10:1-47, 11:19-26, 27-29, 12:5-19, 21-24, 13:1-3, 4-12, 48-52, 14:1-3, 8-11, 21-28, 15:30-34, 16:6-10, 25-34, 17:1-4, 16-21, 33-34, 18:9-11, 24-28, 19:1-10, 11-20, 20:7-12, 27:22-25, 28:1-6, 7-10, 23-24, 39-31).

As earthshaking as God's power was in the first-century Church, there remains today a promise to exceed, in power and glory, the first outpouring of the Holy Spirit. A deeper look into the promise in Joel and the outpouring recorded in book of Acts will unmistakably reveal this truth:

The fullness of the Holy Spirit's outpouring
has been only partially fulfilled!

The promise in Joel does not stop in verse 27, but continues in verses 28, through the end of chapter 4. The Holy Spirit prophesied through Joel that the latter days would see the pouring out of God's Spirit upon His servants with unusual wonders in the heavens and in the earth. According to Joel 2:32, this last great outpouring will include a massive revival throughout the nations of the earth, as well as an enormous movement in the ministry of deliverance. The Lord will baptize the last days' Church with an unusual power to strike against the kingdom of darkness and against the powers of hell.

One prominent feature of this great, latter-day movement will be the people of Israel turning once again to the Lord, at last recognizing Jesus as their promised Messiah. The Apostle Peter reiterates this in Acts 2:19-21. Here again, Peter agrees with Joel, that the outpouring of the Holy Spirit will include unusual wonders in the heavens above and signs on the earth below. Unusual wonders and signs will include blood and fire in vapors of smoke, the sun being turned into darkness, and the moon being turned into blood. It is a direct description of the day of the Lord, when Christ returns to the earth at His second coming. This clearly indicates that a greater measure of the Holy Spirit's baptism outpouring is yet to come, just prior to the coming of the Lord (Joel 19-21, Isaiah 13:9-10, Matthew 24:29-31, Revelation 6:12).

We can, therefore, truly agree:
God has saved the best wine for last!

You and I will have the privilege of partaking in the greatest event in all of Church history. Should the Lord tarry, we are given additional opportunity and a mandate to raise up a generation that is prepared to walk in everything God has promised them. We have the responsibility to train them to be positioned correctly and to walk in the fear of the Lord, having their hearts consecrated to Him, walking in the great commandment of a loving God with all their heart, mind, soul, and strength. Young and old alike, side-by-side, will be a radical, abandoned generation consumed by the zeal of the Lord to see the agenda of Heaven manifested throughout all the earth. What an honor to be living in such a time as this!

It is, therefore, critical for us to allow the Holy Spirit to take us deeper into the heart of God, allowing Him to open up our eyes and ears, to see and hear, with clarity, what He desires. *The hour is late! The hour is urgent!* The Church must have a fresh encounter with the power of the Holy Spirit if we are to contend against the powers of darkness, which will continue to increase its influence of wickedness and depravity throughout all the earth (Matthew 13:24-30).

The last days' outpouring of God's Spirit will not only be marked with great power, but also with great judgment. As darkness increases upon the nations of the earth, the hearts of mankind will be fixated on all kinds of perversions, unimaginable to even consider. The influence of demonic powers in that day will force God's hand of swift justice to sweep through the earth in order to cleanse the earth of all wickedness and to establish the Kingdom of God, advancing into the new millennial reign of Christ. It is a bittersweet moment, nonetheless, necessary, if we are to see righteousness established in the nations of the earth (Isaiah 13:9-13, 24:21-23, Joel 2:30-32, Matthew 24:29-31, Luke 21:25, Acts 2:19-21, Revelation 6:12-17).

> "Behold, the day of the Lord comes, cruel, with both wrath and fierce anger, to lay the land desolate; and He will destroy its sinners from it. For the stars of Heaven and their constellations will not give their light; the sun will be darkened in its going forth, and the moon will not cause its light to shine."
> —*Isaiah 13:9-10*

How can we prepare for a fresh outpouring of God's Spirit? Since we have tolerated vast neglect of the acknowledgment of the Person of the Holy Spirit, it is necessary for us to re-acquaint ourselves with His Person, work and ministry; we must *become familiar with His heart.* Knowing Him intimately increases our familiarity and cooperation with His power and His anointing.

God wants to use us more than we realize, but because of our own lack of knowledge, we are hindered from being very useful in the hand of the Lord. It is essential, then, to be equipped with the knowledge of what God's Word says about who the Holy Spirit is, His anointing and His nine spiritual gifts.

BELIEVE THE PROMISE OF
RECEIVING THE BAPTISM IN THE HOLY SPIRIT

It all begins here: faith. According to the book of Hebrews, without faith it is impossible to please God. One who longs to be pleasing to the Lord is the one who believes that God rewards the believer who diligently seeks Him for what He has promised (Hebrews 11:6). All of God's promises, including the greatest gift of salvation, can be attained only through faith in what God says. Faith is the currency of Heaven, by which all exchanges are accomplished. Regardless of what we see in the natural, reality in the spiritual realm is a much higher and more genuine way of life. What is currently seen with natural eyes will one day yield to the realm of God, sustained by the life of God, through the operation of faith (2 Corinthians 4:16-18).

The Apostle Peter, speaking by the Spirit of prophecy, made a profound prophetic promise to everyone that repented of sin and were baptized in the name of Christ. To the repentant sinner, the Holy Spirit would come and make His home in the heart, and therefore, qualify the individual to receive the gift of the baptism in the Holy Spirit. This was not a promise made only to those called into full-time ministry, but to everyone who put their faith in Christ and to their children, throughout every generation and strata of society (Acts 2:17, 38-39).

BELIEVE THAT GOD'S HOLY ANOINTING
AND HIS SPIRITUAL GIFTS ARE FOR YOU TODAY

Again, faith is critical before the Holy Spirit is able to flow through us with His anointing and power. Writing to the Corinthians, the Apostle Paul contended with them, that they should not remain ignorant concerning the spiritual gifts (1 Corinthians 12:1). Why would Paul make such a statement, unless it was possible to remain uninformed concerning the gifts? Paul longed to see the churches established in the teachings of God's Word, walking in all the promises

God's Word had given to the Church. It was his consuming passion to make his way to the city of Rome for the express purpose of imparting spiritual gifts to the Roman believers so they would be well established in their faith (Romans 1:11).

Developing an intimate relationship with the Holy Spirit is necessary because He is the one who reveals hidden treasures available to us, according to God's Word and desires (1 Corinthians 2:12). Paul's teachings to the Corinthians helped them to understand the manifestation of the Holy Spirit, given to each and every individual believer who had put their faith and trust in the Lord. Everything pertaining to the Kingdom of God is residing inside of us because the Holy Spirit comes to reside within the heart of every believer. I firmly believe that every Christian has at least one spiritual gift given to them. Whether they believe it or not, it will require faith to see the gifts of God's Spirit manifested and expressed through us.

> "But the manifestation of the Spirit is given to each one for the profit of all: for to one is given the word of wisdom through the Spirit, to another the word of knowledge through the same Spirit, to another faith by the same Spirit, to another gifts of healings by the same Spirit, to another the working of miracles, to another prophecy, to another discerning of spirits, to another different kinds of tongues, to another the interpretation of tongues. But one and the same Spirit works all these things, distributing to each one individually as He wills."
> —*1 Corinthians 12:7-11*

The person of the Holy Spirit is the originator of all these gifts and He distributes to each believer individually, as He chooses. It is our responsibility to discover what God has given to us personally, and then learn to apply faith to the spiritual gifts with which God has graced us.

CULTIVATING DESIRE FOR THE GIFTS OF GOD

Throughout my Christian walk, I have been blessed with a desire, constantly consuming me, to be all that God would have me to be. One of the secrets I have learned is to meditate and dig deeply into areas in which I would like to see God operate in my life. Over the past 30 years I have made it a habit to continually study the anointing and power of God, as well as the manner in which the Holy Spirit interacts with the individual believer. This has helped me significantly to understand the operations of the Spirit, and has produced faith in me to believe He truly wants to use me for God's glory. We can stir up a burning desire to be used by God simply by utilizing our time to study God's spiritual gifts.

In 1 Corinthians 14:1, Paul exhorts the Corinthian believers to pursue love and desire spiritual gifts. He strongly admonishes them to learn how to prophesy and to release the gift of prophecy to one another. Prophecy is a precious gift of exhortation, which releases confirmation and comfort to all its recipients (1 Corinthians 14:1-5, 39).

> *Once we understand how spiritual gifts*
> *operate, great faith and confidence is released*
> *in us to express and manifest these gifts.*

As a matter of fact, our confidence in God creates a major fear in the kingdom of darkness. Satan will do everything in his power to keep us from having faith in the Spirit's willingness to work through us. He knows of the authority Jesus has given us to trample on serpents and scorpions and over all the power of the enemy. The enemy is fully aware of the damaging effects that can be done to the kingdom of darkness by one bold, confident believer who will not fear what satan can throw at them (Luke 10:19-20).

> *Having our hearts truly united in intimacy with the Lord*
> *allows us to walk in agreement with the principles of His*
> *Kingdom and*
> *in the power of His righteousness, found in His word. Our lives*
> *are then consumed with revelation as to the urgency of God's*
> *prophetic time clock and the hour in which we live.*

Stop and think about it for a moment. When we become unreservedly assured of the everlasting love of God toward us, and of His desire to manifest Himself to the world through us, we in return, will abandon ourselves to loving God wholeheartedly. Satan fears the resulting flow of anointing created by a believer's intimacy with God, flowing through us as rivers of living water. This is especially true when our desire to be used by God is motivated by love and for the purpose of rescuing souls and setting captives free. God does not give us spiritual gifts so we can exalt ourselves. He releases His grace upon us, so we can plunder hell, expanding the Kingdom of our God (Matthew 16:18-19). Let us, therefore, seek the Lord, to be empowered afresh by the Spirit's anointing, for the sake of reaching the lost, liberating them from all demonic bondage (Psalm 2:8, Luke 10:2, Acts 16:9-10, 18:9, 27:23-24, 1 Timothy 2:1-4, 1 John 3:8.).

The greatest outpouring of God's manifest presence and power is yet to come. Therefore, let us stir our hearts in faith and believe God that you and I will be right in the middle of what He plans to do.

> "Be glad then, you children of Zion, and rejoice in the Lord your God; for He has given you the former rain faithfully, And He will cause the rain to come down for you—The former rain, and the latter rain in the first month."
>
> *—Joel 2:23*

> "Let us know; let us pursue the knowledge of the Lord. His going forth is established as the morning; He will come to us like the rain, like the latter and former rain to the earth."
>
> *—Hosea 6:3*

> "Ask the Lord for rain in the time of the latter rain. The Lord will make flashing clouds; He will give them showers of rain, Grass in the field for everyone."
>
> *—Zechariah 10:1*

"I received an invitation to surrender to the Lord at the age of seven. The Holy Spirit began to birth in me His desires and longings for my life, but many times I resisted His ways, not knowing of the dangers ahead. With a love that is truly stronger than death, and jealousy as strong as the grave, not relenting to let go of its prey, He began to unfold, through prophecy and dreams, the desires of the Father's heart for me! For many years I have kept record of prophetic words given to me and spoken over my life. Many have taken place, many more are unfolding before my eyes and others are yet to happen!

It is in the secret place of prayer and quieting my soul that the Spirit delights in sharing with me the Father's heart and desires. I dreamt of wasting my life for Him, but never thought of the means He would use to take me into deeper places where dying to self would be a 'must.'

Oh, but I must say, 'It is worth it all!'

In the secret place He shares with us how He feels. In this place, the conditions of the hearts of men are naked before His eyes. It is here that atmospheres are changed, hearts are challenged, revelation and understanding are given to bolster my prayers, prophetic words from His heart are uttered through my mouth and power to conquer evil is at hand. I dare not lose this love that keeps me alive and strengthens me to fulfill the desires of His heart! By no means can I say that I have attained perfection, but this one thing I do: I keep pressing on for the high call so that I may be able to meet with Him face to face. I have no greater reward in this life and the one to come than to minister to His heart at His feet and pour my life out as a pleasing aroma before the One that loves my soul!"

—A.C. Full-time Intercessory Missionary
Orlando House of Prayer

Section Six:

Intercession's Power—"Lord, Show Me How To Be Ready!"

I have always been a praying man, but this encounter showed me that I was lacking much in my prayer life by not understanding intercession's governing power in the universe. My prayer life increased dramatically as the Holy Spirit, bit by bit, began to unveil to me the open door and invitation into His throne room. He wanted me to share in His authority and glory.

Chapter 14

God's Delegated Authority Through Prayer

T he Church is being stirred to seek the Holy Spirit's empowerment to stand strong in the trying days of darkness and opposition that will surely be upon us. Proper alignment in Him will cause the Church to operate in power and authority, through the ministry of intercessory worship and prayer. As a result, the Church will find herself positioned as the liaison between Heaven and Earth, to release the will of God upon the nations of the earth. The impact of our prayers will manifest in releasing justice as the Church begins to operate in the power of night-and-day prayer. Our Lord, Himself, emphasized night-and-day prayer as a necessity in preparation for the full release of His justice in every city of the earth. It will be the culmination of all the prayers of the saints that will begin to alter the spiritual atmosphere over cities and nations.

> "And shall God not avenge His own elect who cry out day
> and night to Him, though He bears long with them?"
>
> *—Luke 18:7*

THE NEED FOR NIGHT-AND-DAY PRAYER

In Luke 18 Jesus tells the parable of a persistent widow who was seeking justice from a judge in her city. At first, the judge completely disregarded the widow's need, but due to her continual persistency in coming before him, he finally gave in to her request; her continual coming began to weary him. The Lord used this parable to reveal to His followers the power of continual prayer, coming not before an unjust judge, but a righteous Judge, who sits over the affairs of man and rules over the universe. The lesson given to us here is clearly found in the first verse of the chapter, where Jesus admonishes that men should continually pray and not lose heart, or be discouraged from praying, but approach God in faith. Jesus promises that our prayers will be heard from the Lord, as He assures us of His faithfulness to answer the prayers of His people. It is interesting to note, Jesus shared this parable after teaching about the coming Kingdom of God in the context of turbulent times, eventually leading to the second-coming of our Lord. In other words, God's ability to make wrong things right, releasing judgment and punishment on the rebellious who resist God's justice and bringing salvation to the nations of the earth, will correlate directly with the increase of night-and-day prayer in the days prior to Jesus' return.

The writings of the Old Testament prophets clearly give us a picture of a day when God's Kingdom will be established in all the earth. I believe the Holy Spirit is beginning to reveal to the Church the authority that has been granted to us. We simply need to believe in the identity He has given to us as God's house of prayer and believe in our integral role in bringing about justice through the ministry of intercession.

Two of the main duties of a priest in the Old Testament were to minister primarily, first and foremost, to God in worship and adoration and then to minister to God's people by offering up prayers on their behalf (Exodus 28:1-4, 29:38-46, Deuteronomy 33:10-11, Psalm 141:2, Revelation 5:8). Israel was not faithful in carrying out the responsibilities of her priesthood so God sent her into exile as she experienced His judgments for failing to stand before the Lord in the her priestly office of worship and intercession. (Jeremiah 1:15-16, Malachi 3:2-3).

However, the End-Time Church will walk in a measure of revelation that will cause her to fulfill her spiritual, priestly duties in agreement to God's will and in submission to His leadership. This will release a measure of authority in prayer not seen since the days of Moses and the days of the apostles. The effect of the Church's prayers prior to the coming of the Lord will bring about an awakening in the Church overall, leading to true revival and causing the Church to reach out to the lost in a great world-wide, massive effort of evangelism.

Prior to the coming of the Lord, the Church will begin to see judgment on the compromising, religious spirit that is upon her. Laws and legislations will be affected as God will begin to right the wrongs committed against the poor and helpless. The Church's prayers will begin to affect the ungodly governments and leaders that rule over the nations of the earth. We will begin to see a tremendous move, emphasizing God's holiness and a great display of His anger against the sins of pornography, human trafficking, the drug industry, and all other forms of sin that oppose His righteousness.

A massive, supernatural movement of God's judgment against sickness and infirmity will be seen in the manifestation of God's healing power, operating through His people with great boldness and confidence in the works of the Holy Spirit. These, among other expressions of His justice, are written throughout the books of the prophets and the book of Revelation. Even our Lord's teachings about the end times gives us insight as to what will characterize those days and His plans for manifesting His Father's Kingdom (Matthew 22:1-14, 24:1-51, 25:1-46, 28:18-20, Mark 13:1-37, 14:3-9, 16:14-20, Luke 21:7-36, 24:44-49, Acts 1:3-11).

GOD'S GOVERNMENT IS RELEASED THROUGH THE CORPORATE COOPERATION OF THE CHURCH'S INTERCESSION

As we have seen in chapters five and six, intimacy with God creates a partnership with Him, whereby God can release His governing power through His people as they faithfully operate in the ministry of intercession. Unfortunately, some in the Church do not believe it is necessary to cooperate with God in intercession. They rightly believe that Jesus paid the price for the penalty of our sins, our very ransom, and that He overcame satan. However, they believe, in error, that all we have to do is continue to trust God until He Himself manifests the Kingdom of God. This is an unbiblical way of trusting His sovereignty as this does not empower us, as He intends, to cooperate with Him in the role He has assigned to the Church. This kind of unbiblical trust in God presumes God will do our part, when scripture clearly reveals what has been assigned to us.

The book of Hebrews sheds some light on this truth by showing us that the entire universe is upheld by the power of God's Word (Hebrews 1:3).

Understanding this, we realize the importance of Jesus' instruction to His disciples. He taught them how to effectively abide in Him by allowing His Word to abide in their hearts. The result of this will be a great confidence in us as we approach the Lord in the place of prayer.

> "If you abide in Me, and My words abide in you, you will ask what you desire, and it shall be done for you."
>
> *—John 15:7*

> "Now this is the confidence that we have in Him, that if we ask anything according to His will, He hears us. And if we know that He hears us, whatever we ask, we know that we have the petitions that we have asked of Him."
>
> *—1 John 5:14-15*

We see then, God values the ministry of intercession and prayer. He puts great emphasis on the Church standing upon the promises of God's Word when approaching Him with our prayers. Our prayers are not meant to be arbitrary words, thoughtlessly thrown together. There are prayers that can be filled with words of fear, words of anxiety, words of doubt, and words of unbelief. However, when the Church understands the eternally offered prayers of Jesus Himself, to His Father, through His high-priestly office (Hebrews 7:24-27), we begin to value the priestly ministry that has been bestowed upon us as priests of the Lord. We will be accepted, as we boldly enter into His presence, because of the faithful priestly ministry of Jesus, with which the Heavenly Father is pleased (Hebrews 4:16, Revelation 1:6).

Eventually, as the Church begins to grow in her priestly identity, she will notice intercession giving legal entry points for angels to become more active in the natural realm of mankind.

Depending on the choices we make as believers in the earth, or whether we are fully walking in the delegated authority given to us, we can determine exactly how much activity the kingdom of darkness is allowed to express and manifest throughout the earth. We, as human beings, can either allow demonic activity or angelic activity into our lives and throughout the cities in which we live.

When Jacob the patriarch left Isaac and Rebecca, his father and mother, and fled from his brother Esau, he chose to rest from his flight in a place he named Bethel. As he slept, he had a dream. He saw a ladder, set up on the earth, and its top reached to Heaven. Upon this ladder he saw the angels of God ascending and descending. Above the ladder, he saw the Lord standing. The Lord spoke promises to Jacob and to his descendants, assuring Jacob He would be with him throughout his life, guaranteeing his safety through the word of His promise. Jacob awoke and realized there was an open portal between Heaven and Earth, where spiritual activity could be accessed (Genesis 28:10-22).

The book of Revelation confirms that in the last days, much of mankind will be given over to the worship of demons and all sorts of idols. This clearly gives access to the powers of darkness that seek to interact with humans in order to deceive humanity, bring destruction to their lives, and empower those willing to fully surrender their bodies for the purpose of allowing darkness to increase its reign in the earth (Revelation 9:20, 13:4-18). The Kingdom of Heaven visits the earth through yielded earthen vessels, just as the kingdom of darkness does through vessels not consecrated to God. The choice is ours as to what type of vessel we are.

UNDERSTANDING HOW CORPORATE WORSHIP AFFECTS THE HEAVENS

It's unfortunate that when we meet for our weekly Sunday morning services or midweek services, many remain completely oblivious to the power our corporate praise and worship releases in every city where God's people are gathered. If the Church was to truly understand the power of corporate unity in the presence of God, we would not neglect the opportunity of coming together for the purpose of intercession and lifting up the Name of our Lord. Our weekly church services give us that opportunity 52 weeks out of the year, to release our delegated authority through what I call, "corporate intercessory worship."

We must be reminded of the divine battle tactic that Joshua and his armies used to overthrow the city of Jericho. Joshua sent the priests of the Lord before all of the Israelites, sounding aloud their trumpets, while the rest of the people followed, shouting aloud in praise to God (Joshua 6:1-16). We should remember the Spirit of the Lord coming upon David when he played his harp to relieve King Saul from demonic oppression (1 Samuel 16:14-23). We must not forget how the Prophet Elisha tapped into the prophetic anointing. He would have a minstrel play before him and as the music went forth, the Lord would come upon Elisha and speak through him (2 Kings 3:15).

One of my favorite stories, revealing the power of corporate praise and prayer, is found in II Chronicles 20, where we find the people of Moab, Ammon, and other enemies of Judah, gathered against King Jehoshaphat for battle. King Jehoshaphat was informed of the impending attack, so he set himself to seek the Lord and proclaimed a fast throughout all Judah. The Bible clearly states that all of Judah gathered together and sought help from the Lord. They humbled themselves in His sight and confessed their inability and weakness to withstand the great multitude that was coming against them. God saw their humility and spoke to them through a prophetic word from Jahaziel, who was a Levite and one of the sons of Asaph, a prophetic worshiper in the tabernacle of David. Jahazel prophesied precisely. He said the enemy would approach Judah, but King Jehoshaphat and his army would simply need to stand still and see the salvation of the Lord, Who would be with them in the battle.

There is a powerful lesson here: *We can observe exactly what it means to position ourselves and to stand still and see the salvation of the Lord.* This does not mean we are to be inactive, expecting God's sovereignty to just do everything for us without our participation. The truth of this lesson is that as we position ourselves and stand before Him in our priestly office by releasing praise and prayers to our God, He is faithful to do His part. He will release His angelic forces to confuse our enemies, scattering the powers of darkness.

It is clear to me from this and other examples in Scripture that Jehoshaphat and Judah were given victory because they chose to trust in God's power. They learned how to release it through their obedience in coming before the Lord early in the morning, to praise Him with their voices loud and high. They sang praises to the Lord and glorified the beauty of His holiness as they went out before the foot soldiers proclaiming, *"The Lord is worthy; His mercy endures forever."* God responded by setting ambushes against the people of Moab and Ammon, bringing about a great confusion in their camps; somehow, they fought against each other and destroyed themselves (2 Chronicles 20:1-30).

Another favorite story of mine, showing the power of God's people coming into agreement with Him in the ministry of prayer, is when the king of Assyria, Sennacherib, came against King Hezekiah and Jerusalem, threatening to destroy the city and exile all those from Judah. King Hezekiah responded by crying out to God in prayer and was joined by the Prophet Isaiah. Again, God responded by releasing an angel of the Lord to go into the camp of the Assyrians, killing 185,000 of Judah's enemies (2 Kings 19:14-35, 2 Chronicles 32:20-22). From each of these biblical accounts, we clearly see the role we, as members of the Body of Christ, can play by coming into agreement and walking in our priestly anointing, coming before the Lord with our prayers and our worship. We are able to affect the spiritual atmosphere over our lives and our cities, thereby releasing God's power to bring about a great victory over our spiritual enemies.

> "Let the high praises of God be in their mouth, and a two-edged sword in their hand, to execute vengeance on the nations, And punishments on the peoples; to bind their kings with chains, And their nobles with fetters of iron; to execute on them the written judgment—This honor have all His saints. Praise the Lord!"
>
> —*Psalm 149:6-9*

UNDERSTANDING HOW CORPORATE PRAYER ASSEMBLIES AFFECT IMPENDING CRISIS

> "Now, therefore,' says the Lord, 'Turn to Me with all your heart, with fasting, with weeping, and with mourning. So rend your heart, and not your garments; return to the Lord your God, For He is gracious and merciful, slow to anger, and of great kindness; And He relents from doing harm.

Who knows if He will turn and relent, and leave a blessing behind Him—a grain offering and a drink offering For the Lord your God? Blow the trumpet in Zion, Consecrate a fast, Call a sacred assembly; gather the people, sanctify the congregation, assemble the elders, Gather the children and nursing babes; let the bridegroom go out from his chamber, and the bride from her dressing room.'"

—Joel 2:12-16

One of God's primary calls to a nation in crisis is for the Church to gather together in solemn assemblies for the purpose of praying, worshiping, and fasting. God's people are instructed in Scripture to gather together in corporate unity, so repentance may take place as the people choose to humble themselves before God. If the nations of the earth would learn to turn to God with all their heart, God would respond favorably to that people. The Prophet Joel defined turning to God as returning to the Lord with one's whole heart and with true repentance for sins that are separating us from our God. When Joel saw the impending judgment upon Israel from the up-and-rising power of the Chaldeans (who would eventually destroy Jerusalem and exile all those from Judah), he raised his voice as a loud trumpet to warn the people of their need to respond correctly to the impending judgment God would release through Israel's enemies.

Prayer without true, heartfelt repentance does nothing but exhaust oneself in releasing empty words, with no power before God. The Bible reveals God to be a God of great mercy, Who is longsuffering and does not quickly release His anger when we sin against Him. His nature is to relent from doing harm, but He must have a proper response from His people. For this reason, He raises up prophetic messengers, or forerunners, who will speak on His behalf, warning God's people and the nations of the earth of potential judgment, which could come as a result of rebellion and insistent sin. He raises up people like Joel, who tell the people that *God is looking for our hearts to be rent and not our outer garments.* He raises up intercessors like Abraham, who stood in the gap for the people of Sodom and Gomorrah after the angel of the Lord revealed God's plan to bring destruction upon these two wicked cities (Genesis 19:1-29). He revealed Himself to King Solomon and spoke to him of the power God's people could display in prayer. During this time, God had shut up the heavens, withholding rain. He even commanded the land to be devoured through pestilence because of the sins of the people, but He spoke to Solomon and gave him a divine prescription to bring healing to the nation.

"If My people who are called by My name will humble themselves, and pray and seek My face, and turn from their wicked ways, then I will hear from heaven, and will forgive their sin and heal their land."

—*2 Chronicles 7:14*

Over and over again, our merciful God raises up servants to prophesy the heart of God to His people who have become distant and divided in their hearts against Him. Abraham, Moses, Samuel, Jeremiah, Daniel, Ezekiel, Amos, Zephaniah, Habakkuk, Jonah, Malachi, and others were known to cry out on behalf of God to restore a backslidden people so His wrath would be averted. We have been given an incredible gift to be able to come before our God with worship and prayer, representing the people of the earth through the priestly anointing He has placed upon us. Oh, may the Church in this hour receive the revelation of our need to come together as one people and beckon the Lord to be merciful to us and to our land, which is in desperate need of justice and righteousness. We must humble ourselves before our God and obey what Scripture clearly reveals to us, turn from our sins, and return to our God. Who knows exactly how much of God's anger and displeasure can be stayed back, if we walk in the authority as His intercessors?

"Gather yourselves together, yes, gather together, O undesirable nation, before the decree is issued, or the day passes like chaff, before the Lord's fierce anger comes upon you, Before the day of the Lord's anger comes upon you! Seek the Lord, all you meek of the earth, who have upheld His justice. Seek righteousness; seek humility. It may be that you will be hidden in the day of the Lord's anger."

—*Zephaniah 2:1-3*

"For numerous years we have prayerfully stood in the gap of intercession between God and man, on behalf of the needs of many people. We thought we knew most of what was required to be «Intercessors». Since coming to the Orlando House of Prayer, where intimacy with Jesus, prayer, and the Word of God are as much a priority as breathing, we have learned the true meaning of authority in corporate prayer and intercession. Our prayers and intercession are no longer fueled only by people's needs, crises, and casualties. Rather, they are fueled by our intimate relationship with Jesus, as our Bridegroom King and the life-giving Word of God, which postures our hearts and lives to walk in authoritative partnership in prayer as a part of the corporate Body of Christ, and with Jesus Himself, Who is our Great High Priest.

We have learned that the awesome authority of corporate worship and warfare in intercession is always based on the authority of God's Word, as it is written, and then prayed out of a pure, worshipping heart that has been captivated by the intimate, living Word of God—Jesus Christ. Musicians and prayer leaders blend worship and prayer together as we individually receive fresh downloads from heaven. We produce a single, harmonized sound in one beautiful, authoritative, earth-shaking, life-changing voice. A collective cry reaches the sanctuary of the Lord's heavenly temple, incense rises before His throne, and He uses our intercession, in agreement with His Word, to bring about His very will and purposes in the earth.

The authority of corporate intercession establishes the government of God in the earth, just as it is in heaven."

—Rick & Chyrl Watts
Full-time Intercessory Missionaries
Orlando House of Prayer

Chapter 15

Agreeing With God to Shift the Heavens

God's Word has much to say about the urgent need for intercession. His purpose is for night-and-day prayer to go forth from the Church throughout the earth. The Lord Himself gives us a bit of insight into the heart of the Father, concerning night-and-day prayer. In Luke 11 the disciples asked our Lord a very important question: *"Would you teach us to pray?"*

Let me just say, on a side note, if I had been given the opportunity to ask the Lord any question, quite possibly my question could have been more like one of these: *"Lord, can you teach me how to heal the sick the way you do?" "What is the secret to having such authority against the kingdom of darkness?" "Can you show me how to raise the dead?"* Or, I might have asked Him, *"How do you do one of those supernatural miracles, like walking on water or commanding the sea to be calm?"* If I were in the position as one of His 12 disciples, I don't know for sure what I might have asked Him, but would I have asked Him, *"Teach me to pray?"*

When we observe what the disciples perceived in Jesus' relationship with His heavenly Father, we might understand their request better. Think about it. They were spending time with the creator God, and they had the opportunity to ask Him anything, and they decided to ask Him about connecting with God in prayer. This is absolutely astounding, and makes me wonder about the powerful impact Jesus must have made in the lives of His disciples in how He expressed His relationship with God, the Father. Jesus' band of followers must have detected something enticing about His interaction in communion with God. Jesus was extremely different from any other man they had ever known. He was full of compassion, mercy, and long-suffering; His life was marked with the spirit of zeal, and He was filled with joy. They might have wondered if His behavior and character had any correlation to the intimate relationship they knew He had with God.

ETERNAL ONENESS

From the beginning of God's revelation to man, the Scriptures describe God as One who initiates and seeks out man to commune and fellowship with him. In the book of Genesis, we see the Lord creating man in the image and likeness of Himself (Genesis 1:26). This wonderfully reveals the purpose for which man was created: *to satisfy God's craving for love and fellowship, found only through having intimate relationship with the Godhead.*

The nature of God is oneness. That is to say, there is a perfect union between the Father, the Son, and the Holy Spirit. Jesus reveals this truth in His priestly prayer for His disciples and for any who would believe in Him. He prayed they would experience the same perfect unity as the Father and the Son have experienced from eternity (John 17:21-24). It was a prayer of oneness and of perfect intimacy, expressing Jesus' longing to experience it eternally with His disciples. It is safe to say then, the revelation we see in the book of Genesis is a clear description of God as One who seeks out man Moreover, when Jesus is asked by His disciples to teach them how to pray and seek God, His response should come as no surprise to us. In it, He revealed the true purpose and nature of prayer.

Rather than creating a list of rules and regulations, or introducing a mentality of works, Jesus' first revelation about approaching God in prayer was for us to realize that God is more than just a Creator. He is, first and foremost, a Father! What does this reveal? It discloses much about the heart of God and His genuine stirring of passion and compassion for His people. Revelation of God, as Father, makes Him known to us as a God who is approachable, One who desires for mankind to encounter Him.

Furthermore, such comprehension declares the sovereignty of God, for He rules and reigns from heaven. We are secure in Him, knowing His tender care is watching over all of God's children. Jesus is qualified to communicate this truth because He is the perfect picture of God in the flesh. Fully God and fully man, Jesus came to proclaim what was in the heart of the Father to a lost humanity, so that perfect union between God and man could be restored.

ON EARTH AS IT IS IN HEAVEN

"Now it came to pass, as He was praying in a certain place, when He ceased, that one of His disciples said to Him, 'Lord, teach us to pray, as John also taught his disciples.' So He said to them, 'When you pray, say: Our Father in heaven, hallowed be Your name. Your Kingdom come. Your will be done. On earth as it is in heaven."

—Luke 11:1-2

With God as our Father, ruling and reigning from heaven above, how can we, human beings on earth, connect with Him exactly—no more, no less—as He desires for us to do so? Exactly what did Jesus mean when He said, God's Kingdom must come, and His will needs to be accomplished on earth, as it is in heaven? Moses and David both received prophetic revelations into the spiritual activity of heaven. This is why each of them were given detailed directives for the construction of a tent; the former known as the "Tabernacle of Moses" and the latter as the "Tabernacle of David." This was God's prophetic insight to us, tuning us into the atmosphere of Heaven, as well as showing us how humanity has been invited to interact with the presence and glory of God.

The instructions given to Moses were clear and concise, in accordance to a pattern God had given to him. This earthly tabernacle was to be patterned after the heavenly tabernacle so that God would be able to dwell among His people. Here again, we see the heart of the Lord and His desire for companionship with humanity. Everything about the tabernacle that Moses built was for the divine purpose of interacting and fellowshipping with man.

"And let them make Me a sanctuary, that I may dwell among them. According to all that I show you, that is, the pattern of the tabernacle and the pattern of all its furnishings, just so you shall make it."

—Exodus 25:8-9

"And you shall put it before the veil that is before the ark of the Testimony, before the mercy seat that is over the Testimony, where I will meet with you. Aaron shall burn on it sweet incense every morning; when he tends the lamps, he shall burn incense on it. And when Aaron lights the lamps at twilight, he shall burn incense on it, perpetual incense before the Lord throughout your generations."

—Exodus 30:6-8

In a very similar way, the Lord encountered the heart of David and unmistakably gave him prophetic direction through the prophets Nathan and Gad, who were instrumental in helping David know God's will for his personal life, as well as the kingdom of Israel. Like Moses, David was instructed to erect a tent to house the Ark of the Covenant, which was the place where the glory of God resided among His people. Unlike Moses' tabernacle, which involved much furniture, symbolizing spiritual truths as to the manner in which God could be approached, David's tabernacle housed only the Ark of the Covenant. Other furnishings were replaced by the activity of the Levites who ministered to the Lord through song and music.

In David's tabernacle, there was no brazen altar (blood sacrifices), water of laver (washing for the priests), candlesticks (to give light in the Holy Place), table of showbread (12 loaves of bread), or altar of incense (sweet incense to burn before the Lord). All of these furnishings were found only in the Tabernacle of Moses and were completely replaced in David's tabernacle. All of the truths that were represented by these furnishings could be experienced by the presence of the Lord. I believe the revelation David had about the presence of the Lord actually caused him to be a man addicted to God. He was known to be a man after God's own heart, and David's life reflected God's consuming passion (Psalm 27:4, 8-9, 63:1-3, 73:25-26, Acts 13:22). Therefore, the Lord revealed to David just how the average Israelite would be given access into the presence of the Lord.

"Then David gave his son Solomon the plans for the vestibule, its houses, its treasuries, its upper chambers, its inner chambers, and the place of the mercy seat; and the plans for all that he had by the Spirit, of the courts of the house of the Lord, of all the chambers all around, of the treasuries of the house of God, and of the treasuries for the dedicated things."

—1 Chronicles 28:11-12

"And he stationed the Levites in the house of the Lord with cymbals, with stringed instruments, and with harps, according to the commandment of David, of Gad the king's seer, and of Nathan the prophet; for thus was the commandment of the Lord by His prophets."

—2 Chronicles 29:25

Understanding the significance of the "Tabernacle of Moses" and the "Tabernacle of David" is beneficial to the average believer today because through these two great servants of God, we possess prophetic awareness of coming humbly, boldly, and rightfully before the presence of the Lord. This is the very reason Jesus told us to pray for the activity of Heaven to be replicated in the earth. He wanted us to know that we have access.

About 250 years after King David, God raised up a fiery prophet by the name of Isaiah. Isaiah's calling into the prophetic ministry was marked by a profound encounter. Isaiah was overwhelmed, captured by the presence of God, and he remained faithful throughout his prophetic ministry, devoted to the calling upon his life. Like Moses and David, Isaiah also saw a pattern in Heaven. This time, though, the pattern involved actual angelic beings, above and near the throne of the Lord where He was seated.

These angelic creatures would continually cry out, "Holy, Holy, Holy is the Lord of hosts! The whole earth is full of his glory!"
(Isaiah 6:3)

As they exalted the Lord, the entryway into the throne of God would be shaken by the resounding power of the praise and worship toward God from His heavenly creatures.

Later in history, like Isaiah, the Apostle John was given revelation into the actual activity of Heaven surrounding the throne of God. John not only saw heavenly creatures, he also saw human beings taking their places around the throne as they joined in with the heavenly creatures, worshiping the Lord. They were clothed in white garments (symbolic of the righteous acts of the saints) and wore golden crowns (symbolic of an authoritative position in God). Before them and around the throne were living creatures, giving glory and honor and thanks to the Lord. As the living creatures worshiped Him, the 24 elders fell down before the throne and joined in the worship of Heaven, casting down their golden crowns before Him saying, *"Worthy are You, oh Lord, to receive glory, honor, and power; for You have created all things and for Thy pleasure they are created."*

> "Around the throne were twenty-four thrones, and on the thrones I saw twenty-four elders sitting, clothed in white robes; and they had crowns of gold on their heads . . . Before the throne there was a sea of glass, like crystal. And in the midst of the throne, and around the throne, were four living creatures full of eyes in front and in back . . . Whenever the living creatures give glory and honor and thanks to Him who sits on the throne, who lives forever and ever, the twenty-four elders fall down before Him who sits on the throne and worship Him who lives forever and ever, and cast their crowns before the throne, saying: 'You are worthy, O Lord, To receive glory and honor and power; For You created all things, and by Your will they exist and were created.'"
>
> —*Revelation 4:4, 6, 9-11*

John's revelation was a very similar scene to the one the Prophet Isaiah saw, except John portrayed it with greater understanding and interpreted it with more lucidity. This is how prophetic revelation works: God seals spiritual truths in one generation and then He reveals it with greater clarity in another generation (Daniel 12:4, 8-9). John's revelation really stands out to me. In fact, this particular revelation has drastically transformed my life and completely altered the way we conduct our ministry here at the Orlando House of Prayer.

THE END TIME REVELATION OF 24/7 PRAYER AND WORSHIP

> "The four living creatures, each having six wings, were full of eyes around and within. And they do not rest day or night, saying: "Holy, holy, holy, Lord God Almighty, Who was and is and is to come!"
>
> —*Revelation 4:8*

John not only saw both angels and redeemed humanity worshiping the Lord around the throne, but he also saw it taking place day and night continually, never ceasing and never resting. John was witnessing 24/7 worship taking place in Heaven. As the vision of John continued to evolve, he beheld an increase of activity surrounding the throne room of the Lord. In addition to continual worship, John saw the worship coming from the saints mixed with their prayers. Continual worship and prayer had not been seen clearly in any of the previous pattern revelations, although it was indicated in the revelation Moses received when he was instructed to make an altar on which the priests were to burn incense perpetually (Exodus 30:1, 7-8).

In the Old Testament, the burning of incense was done in the Holy Place, which was an inner room inside the tabernacle where incense was to be burned and offered up to God on the Altar of Incense. The altar was located just in front of the Ark of the Covenant, according to the instruction of the Lord, which He had revealed to Moses. (Exodus 30:6). As incense would burn, the smoke created would rise, symbolic of the prayers of the saints, coming up before the Lord, as a sweet smelling sacrifice (Psalm 141:2). Clearly, this is a spiritual lesson as to God's intention to meet with His people as they come before Him with their worship and their prayers.

> "Now when He had taken the scroll, the four living creatures and the twenty-four elders fell down before the Lamb, each having a harp, and golden bowls full of incense, which are the prayers of the saints."
>
> —*Revelation 5:8*

> "And the smoke of the incense, with the prayers of the saints, ascended before God from the angel's hand."
>
> —*Revelation 8:4*

THE INTERCESSORS' AUTHORITY WITH GOD

Throughout the Bible, God has been consistent in using His servants as the integral instrument to shift nations and change key circumstances, moving the hand of God through the power of prayer. God has chosen the vehicle of prayer as the means in which He will govern the universe and release His will upon the nations of the earth. For intercession to have its full effect there must be intercessors, those who are willing to come boldly before the Lord. Intercessors cooperate with God like Abraham, who was able to stand before the Lord, crying out on behalf of the righteous remaining in Sodom and Gomorrah. Intercessors like Aaron, the high priest, plead with God when His anger is burning hotly against the people. Aaron stood between the Lord and the people, burning incense in order to stop the plague of destruction from annihilating the Israelites (Genesis 18:16-23, Numbers 16:44-48).

Others, like Moses (Exodus 32:10-14), Daniel (Daniel 9:1-19), the Church of Acts (Acts 4:23-31, 12:5-9, 13:1-3), and the Apostle Paul (Ephesians 1:15-23, Philippians 1:9-11, Colossians 1:9-11), were all used mightily through their lives of prayer and their influence with God. Therefore, it is no surprise to see that prior to the Lord's coming God will again turn to the Church as the instrument to partner with Him, releasing the 21 judgments in the book of Revelation, to bring about the destruction and the end of the antichrist's reign. It is, moreover, no doubt that the Lord is orchestrating a worldwide prayer movement in all of the nations of the earth in preparation for the second coming of Christ.

Never before, in all of history, has there been such a worldwide emphasis on worship, fasting, and intercession. This is an explicit, prophetic sign that the Holy Spirit is preparing God's people for the greatest movement and out-pouring of the Spirit's activity on the face of the earth. The book of Revelation clearly depicts a Church fully engaged with the spirit of intercession, mani-festing the will of God on the earth. The release of each of the seven seals, the seven trumpets and the seven bowls of judgment is preceded by the activity of worship and intercession (Revelation 5:8-6:1, Revelation 8:1-6, Revelation 15:1-16:1). I believe with all of my heart that this is the reason God's Spirit is raising up houses of prayer all across the earth, in every major city, with an emphasis for night-and-day prayer. Churches are beginning to band together to cry out to the Lord as they begin to understand that the only hope for the nations is the Church releasing the greatest authority and power against the kingdom of darkness—such power and authority come only through prayer.

> "If My people who are called by My name will humble themselves, and pray and seek My face, and turn from their wicked ways, then I will hear from Heaven, and will forgive their sin and heal their land."
>
> *—2 Chronicles 7:14*

"I've lived in Ocoee, Florida (just west of Orlando), since 1988 and was called to intercede for this area shortly after that. The Holy Spirit arranged divine introductions with many people to whom He had also issued this call. There have been numerous prayer-walks, prayer-drives, prayer fly-overs, etc., for this fore-runner state and the Orlando area in particular. One amazing initiative that I was privileged to take part in was held in a high crime area of Orlando. This was initiated at the request of the Orlando Chief of Police. After two years of prayer on the streets, the Orlando Police Department publicly acknowledged a 30% drop of crime in this area.

Does prayer shift the heavens? Will there be transformation in the Orlando area? Yes, I know there will be. As 24/7 prayer continues in houses of prayer, the words that have been given to me and to others, such as, 'Orlando is a City of Refuge,' 'Ocoee is the center of Godly Living,' 'Pine Hills will no longer be known as 'crime hills' but as the 'Hills of Light,' are becoming reality.

All of this is happening now. I hear these expressions as people talk in local supermarkets, restaurants, banks, and public gatherings: 'Hallelujah,' 'Praise God,' 'Glory,' and 'Amen,' are becoming a natural part of speech. The armies are being marshaled as many ministries are being called to and being birthed in the area. Keep praying; the heavens are shifting! 'Thy Kingdom come...'"

—Testimony of Judy Chedwick
Full-time Staff
Orlando House of Prayer

179

Facebook:
CarlosSarmientoOHOP

Twitter:
CSarmientoOHOP

Contact:
Carlos@OrlandoHop.org

Other Products from Carlos Sarmiento

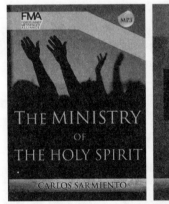

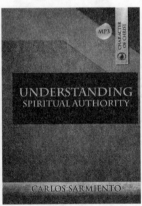

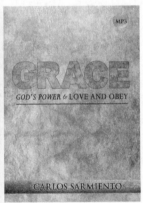

www.OrlandoHop.org